OLD FURNITURE
Understanding the Craftsman's Art

OLD FURNITURE

Understanding the Craftsman's Art

by Nancy A. Smith

Drawings by Glenna Lang · Photographs by Richard Cheek

Little, Brown and Company
Boston   Toronto

To my family,
which has been cajoled, bribed, badgered
and resigned into endurance

Library of Congress Cataloging in Publication Data

Smith, Nancy A.
  Old furniture: understanding the craftsman's art.

  1. Furniture making.   2. Furniture—Repairing.
3. Furniture finishing.   I. Lang, Glenna.   II. Cheek, Richard.   III. Title.
TT200.S55 1976   684.1'04   76-13035
ISBN 0-316-79932-7

For the material on reparation of tables on pages 139 and 140, the author is indebted to Charles H. Hayward's *Furniture Repairs,* published by Evans Brothers, Ltd., London, 1967.

Published simultaneously in Canada
by Little, Brown & Company (Canada) Limited

PRINTED IN THE UNITED STATES OF AMERICA

ACKNOWLEDGMENTS

SO MANY PEOPLE have shown interest in my research project and extended encouragement in various forms. The isolated and long-ago cheers I especially recall at this writing. Each I thank—each knows who he is, and I share the pleasure of this accomplishment with him.

The actual implementation of this book has demanded the assistance, consultation, patience and energies of many more people. I thank them herewith for their generosity:

Mr. Arthur C. Alexander, Royall House; Miss Pauline Allaway; Mrs. Georgia Bumgardner, American Antiquarian Society; Miss Beth Carver; Mr. Vincent Cerbone, Museum of Fine Arts, Boston; Mr. Richard Cheek; Mrs. Paul Coombs; Mr. John Demers; Mr. and Mrs. Edward Dewey; Miss Deborah Emerson; Mr. Jonathan Fairbanks, Museum of Fine Arts, Boston; Miss Etta Falkner, Sturbridge Village; Mr. and Mrs. James Hamill; Mr. Henry Harlow, Sturbridge Village; Mr. Brock Jobe; Miss Patricia Kane, Garvin Collection, Yale University; Miss Glenna Lang; Mr. John W. Melody, Winterthur Museum; Miss Rosalie Moretti; Mr. Marvin Moss, Thonet Industries Inc.; Miss Barbara Neilson; Mrs. Ruth Nickerson; Mr. Richard Nylander, Society for the Preservation of New England Antiquities; Mrs. J. Clifford Ross; Mr. Lawrence Sickman, William Rockhill Nelson Gallery of Art; Dr. and Mrs. Joseph Vargas; Mr. Bron Warsaskas; Mr. Michael Wilson, Victoria and Albert Museum, London; Wu Tung, Museum of Fine Arts, Boston.

CONTENTS

INTRODUCTION

OLD FURNITURE is exciting. Richness of wood figure combined with the mellowness of age have tremendous emotional appeal to most viewers in this age of bustle, space and synthetics. One senses that each old piece is unique, made for one person by another in a time and life-style that we do not know, cannot recapture and thus hold in reverence.

The cabinetmaker of today rarely has the opportunity to create from the magnificent pieces of hardwood used in the past—splendid, huge, richly figured boards, measuring up to three feet in width. An entire 18th century tea table top was frequently made from a single piece of wood. Fine wood such as mahogany, imported from the Caribbean, and used by the cabinetmaker for his best work, was as important a part of 18th century Elegance as the tea and silk imported from the Orient. Even today we can sense and participate in the pleasure the use of the finest materials gave both craftsman and customer alike.

Old furniture is exciting in its design and detail. Which designs and which details most appeal to each individual becomes personal preference but certainly all have been admired in each generation. The fact that furniture reproduction, faking, and the search for the truly old has flourished to the extent that it has during the 19th and 20th centuries indicates the general attraction of old pieces.

A further source of admiration today is the tremendous skill and resourcefulness of yesterday's furniture craftsman working by hand in his shop with hand tools. Occasionally an available furniture design book would suggest ideas and styles, sometimes seeing pieces which had been made elsewhere would alter his planning and encourage new skills, certainly patrons dictated wishes, but each furniture maker in the end made his own contribution. Consider the cabinetmaking skill involved in the creation of this card table top with a rounded corner recessed for candlesticks and an oval pocket for chips, the whole accomplished with a single piece of wood as can be seen by following the continuous wood grain. Because of details employed by certain cabinetmakers, it is possible to recognize, categorize and regionalize individuals and groups of cabinetmakers (the Goddard-Townsend family in Newport, for example). These many combined skills, impressively mastered (or not) brought the piece into being, and we admire and seek out the products of the early cabinetmaker's abilities—something almost gone in our assembly-line society.

A fascinating aspect of old furniture is its history. One can speculate upon who made a particular piece for whom and for what reason or occasion. The circumstances through which a piece has survived to be with us today provoke the imagination. Sometimes it is possible to learn such details

1. Interior of the Dominy Woodworking Shop, East Hampton, New York, now reconstructed at the Winterthur Museum, where the Dominy family of craftsmen worked from about 1760 to about 1840. The cabinetmaker's oak workbench here seen was the center of his activity. Photograph courtesy the Henry Francis du Pont Winterthur Museum.

◀ 2. Rounded corner of mahogany 1730–1750 Boston card table top.

3. *Old Kingdom Egypt mortise and tenon joint from bed canopy of Queen Hetepheres I, showing copper-cased mortise and tenon forming practical bearing surfaces. Photograph courtesy the Museum of Fine Arts, Boston.*

4. *New Kingdom Egypt cedar wood chair with bone and ivory inlays. Photograph courtesy the Brooklyn Museum, Charles Edwin Wilbour Fund.*

by checking family records and doing other kinds of research.

The excitement of old furniture becomes even greater when one recognizes the furniture details and techniques that have come down to us through history. How interesting to realize that the mortise and tenon joint was utilized in Old Kingdom Egypt, 3000 B.C. This is documented by the study of the gold-cased bed canopy, now in the Cairo Museum, found in the tomb of Queen Hetepheres I, mother of Cheops, builder of the Great Pyramid. The Egyptian chair with animal legs and a sloping back (Illustration 4), one of the oldest existing chairs dating from XVIII Dynasty (2000–1500 B.C.) is also constructed with mortise and tenon joints and is fastened with visible pegs.

Earliest Chinese chair and table construction (about 800 A.D., before which the Chinese used mats on the floor) display traditional construction and jointing. No furniture remains extant prior to the 15th century, so pictured here (Illustrations 5 and 6) are a 15th century Chinese table and an early 17th century chair of the Ming Dynasty (1368–1662 A.D.). The table shows the use and appreciation of hardwood for furniture at this early date. Not only was such wood considered beautiful but its hardness and strength allowed designs to be light and graceful. The cabriole leg with the scrolled foot, for example, so universal to 18th century cabinetwork, dates back at least to T'ang Dynasty China (618–907 A.D.). The Chinese also veneered core wood with finer wood sheets of veneer. Note the panel and frame seat construction using mitre-corner mortise and tenon joints on the Ming Dynasty chair. The chair's vase-shaped serpentine splat back

5. *15th century K'ang table of huang-hua li wood (a variety of rosewood) with cabriole legs. Height, 12"; length, 36⅜"; depth, 23". Photograph courtesy private collection.*

highly prized and desired. Given the limited supply and the growing demand, the values and prices paid for ownership continue to rise. This can be clearly seen by visiting antique shops, auction sales, and antique shows as well as by studying the specialized publications. A particularly challenging aspect of the old furniture market is the presence of spurious pieces. The question of faking and how to look for authenticity in an "old" piece will be dealt with at length in this text.

As increasing numbers of people become interested in old furniture, information on how to recognize and judge a given piece would seem very welcome in assisting the new student and collector to appreciate old pieces and buy wisely. During my apprenticeship experience with a cabinetmaker working with old tools in the traditional ways, he encouraged me to explore and discern more and new aspects of old furniture. I come to you with my discoveries up to now, and I hope that they will be helpful and interesting to you as they have been to me.

In the following pages, attempts will be made to train and sharpen the reader's powers of observation and deduction—thereby

and the horseshoe-shaped continuous rail were very important to early 18th century European furniture.

Proof of the excitement of old furniture can be found in the market place. Any market place is intriguing, and the market for old furniture grows increasingly dynamic. Old pieces, genuine to their period of history are enabling him to best recognize the most important rudimentary qualities and features pertinent to handcrafted furniture of wood. We shall analyze many aspects of furniture construction—the interior vs. the exterior of a piece, panelling and moldings, the major joints and where each is used, old nails and screws, the intricacies of wood carving, the significance of planing marks and details of veneering. Furniture finishes will also be examined.

A study of wood movement will be made and its tell-tale signs of movement with time will be investigated. Contrary to much thinking, wood is in a constant state of change regardless of age—it expands and contracts with temperature and humidity changes and it reacts differently depending on the kind and part of the wood used.

Another section of this book will be devoted to the accessories of furniture—its brasses, hinges, locks, casters and glass. These are vital parts of any piece, functional as well as decorative, and provide many clues to the history of a piece. Often they are a source of delight in their creativity, and it is good fun to discover how flamboyant the craftsman could be. In the approach to these accessories, the importance of considering both sides of any given object will be stressed.

6. *17th century Ming Dynasty Continuous Horseshoe Chinese arm chair of huang hua li wood. Courtesy of Robert Hatfield Ellsworth, from his book "Chinese Furniture" (Random House, New York).*

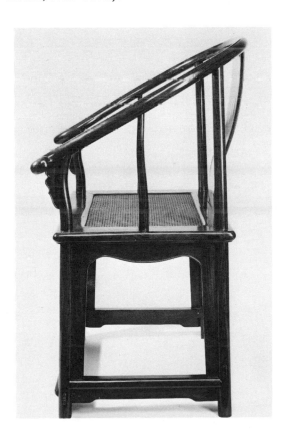

Although this is not always easy to do—locks, for example, are securely embedded in old wood—such study can supply critical information when a piece of furniture falls under suspicion.

In addition to the physical properties of old furniture and how it was made, old pieces shall be considered in terms of what has happened to them with time. A chapter on points of wear examines the aging process and its effects on furniture (sometimes to the extent of actual damage). A chapter will deal with furniture repairs—what repairs and restorations can teach us about the history of a piece and how to identify and evaluate such work.

Once the basic principles of old furniture identification are understood, further refinements and details must be researched and mastered. That is to say, after a piece has been considered in terms of its age characteristics, its construction and condition, attention should be directed to judging the piece as a good representative of its period in terms of style, proportion, material and detail. Provenance is another major consideration. In evaluating a piece, emotion also plays an important role. Opinions vary as to the priority of these various factors.

Weighing these many considerations is an exercise and technique which will constantly improve with repetition and experience. The more practice, the better the conclusion.

FURNITURE MAKING TECHNIQUES

1

WOOD—ITS CHARACTERISTICS AND HOW IT IS WORKED

MAN'S EARLIEST FURNITURE, known to us by its remains or through pictorial data, was made of wood. This is not surprising since wood was readily available, possible to work with the simplest of tools, and served the intended purposes. Furniture construction as such had its beginning when the woodworker ceased making chests by hollowing out tree trunks and making the lids from one thick plank, and instead began banding individual boards with wrought-iron straps and hinging the lids. These hewn chests, predating the 15th century, are the earliest examples of Western furniture in existence today.

As more tools were developed to aid the woodworker and his understanding of his materials increased, stout planks either split or sawn from the log were crudely put together with oak pins or wrought-iron nails at the angles. In the 16th and 17th centuries, chests were joined with joints, such as the mortise and tenon joint and the woodworker involved was called a joiner.

The chest was the earliest form of what we call case furniture today. This category of furniture suggests a case or box kind of construction. Other case pieces include chests of drawers, cabinets, cupboards, desks and sideboards. The other main categories of furniture are chair furniture (including settees and sofas) whose considerations and methods of construction are completely different from case pieces, and table furniture, again having unique construction requirements.

All of these many categories of furniture first became prevalent in the late 17th century and many skills were required of the maker —far beyond the simple jointing of heavy solid wood pieces by the joiner of earlier days. Hence, the "cabinetmaker" became a highly respected craftsman and the names of many are still known today. His skills included jointing, veneering, turning, carving, and gilding the wood. He used both local woods and woods from distant lands which had different properties or were fashionably pleasing.

There are a great many varieties of wood, a number of which have been used in the construction and decoration of furniture. As we have noted, the earliest furniture of the West in existence today in any quantity is of hand-hewn riven oak (i.e., split on its natural cleavage lines with an axe or adze) and dates back to the 15th and 16th centuries. These pieces have survived because oak was available everywhere to be used as a construction material and was so used, and because good quality oak is especially strong and durable.

In the 17th, 18th and 19th centuries, certain woods became fashionable and appropriate for use by cabinetmakers in the making

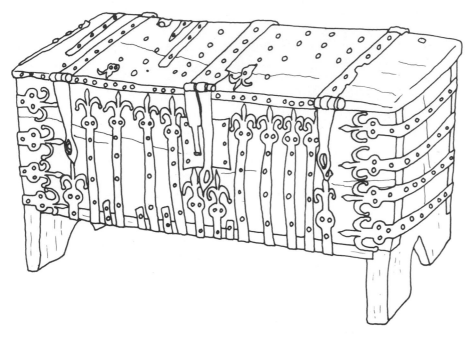

*7. 13th century Rhineland coffer
of hand-hewn oak planks.*

of furniture. One of these was walnut which, with its interesting natural figures, color and decorative burls, contributed to the fashion of veneered furniture during the late 17th and early 18th centuries.

When the West Indies mahoganies were discovered and imports became possible, this closely-grained strong wood lent itself well to the rococo carving and fretwork which became popular during the careers of cabinet-makers such as Chippendale and Shearer in the mid-18th century. The earliest mahoganies adopted and worked, about 1730, were dark and heavy woods without figure and they were worked in the solid, there being no reason to economize on the decorative wood figure by slicing it into veneer sheets. Other mahoganies were finely figured, some with great exuberant plume figures, and thus, veneer furniture construction was again practiced.

Toward the end of the 18th century carving as decoration was replaced by veneers of various woods and inlaid designs. New and exotic woods for veneer work were introduced, many of which were imported from foreign lands. For example, satinwood, much of it from the West Indies, was used more at this time than ever before or since. The work of Hepplewhite and the designs of the Adam Brothers are often representative of this so-called "Age of Satinwood."

Ubiquitous pine, a softwood, was used during these same years as both a primary wood (wood that shows) and as a secondary wood (wood parts not intended to be seen, such as the core wood to which decorative veneer is glued). Other local woods, both hard-woods and soft-woods, were used for furniture construction. The varieties are endless but poplar, maple, cherry, beech, fruit woods, chestnut, ash and yew are frequently encountered. Because of the practicality of using the immediately available, relatively cheap, and familiar local wood, the study of regional woods becomes an interesting method for identifying the geographical area in which a piece of furniture might have been made.

Unfortunately, however, wood was sometimes traded between areas, so that any conclusion at best is speculative. Furthermore, it is extremely difficult many times to decide with certainty what the wood really is. Only micro-analysis of the wood vessels, a laboratory analysis done in a few specialized laboratories such as The Forest Products Laboratory in Madison, Wisconsin, can properly ascertain wood species. Use of local wood for furniture making usually goes hand in hand with solid forms of construction (rather than veneer work) and designs of relative simplicity as compared to high fashion urban pieces made at the same time.

Certain woods, with their own characteristics and properties, influenced styles at different periods of history. And in reverse, the requirements of different fashions and needs brought individual woods into use and prominence. Thus, the Queen Anne style is often referred to as the "Age of Walnut" while the "Age of Mahogany" is synonymous with mid-18th century Georgian and American Colonial furniture. In broad terms this proves a helpful initial approach to identifying furniture. A Chinese Chippendale chair carved in oak, for example, would indeed be a rarity —certainly requiring careful scrutiny before confirmation.

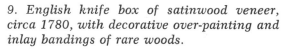

8. *Late 18th century bow-front chest of drawers with drawer fronts of matched plume-figured mahogany veneer.*

9. *English knife box of satinwood veneer, circa 1780, with decorative over-painting and inlay bandings of rare woods.*

WOOD GRAIN

STRAIGHT GRAIN

All wood has grain. Grain refers to the direction and arrangement of the wood elements—the pores and fibers. The natural development of the fibrous elements, sometimes called tracheid vessels, in relation to the axis of growth, results in grain. When the general direction of the elements parallels the direction of growth (from bottom to top of trunk) the grain is *straight grain*. (See illustration 10 for examples of wood grain variations.)

IRREGULAR GRAIN

Due to knots and other irregularities in the wood, deflections occur in the growth of the wood elements producing *irregular grain*.

Other natural causes may alter the straight grain growth resulting in *wavy grain* (horizontal waves), which is often produced in the limb area where compression occurs as the tree trunk and branches expand in their seasonal growths; *spiral grain*, when the elements twist; *interlocked grain*, when the elements of successive growth rings twist in alternate directions as they grow upward; and *silver grain*, which contains flecks or broader and longer markings produced by wood rays.

SMOOTH AND ROUGH GRAIN

In addition to its character and direction, grain may be either smooth or rough depending on whether the fibers have remained flat and unbroken in the cutting and planing of the wood or whether they have lifted and frayed during these operations.

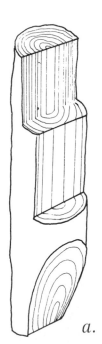 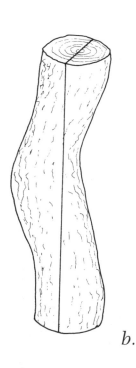 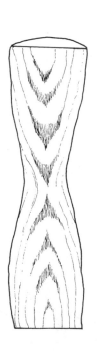 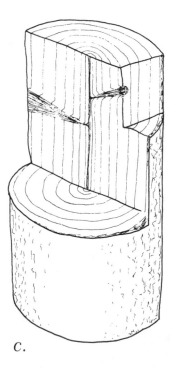

a.   *b.*   *c.*

10. *Wood Grain Variations*

a. A log cut from different angles causes the straight grain appearance to vary.

b. A curved log cut straight produces wood grain of parabola figure.

c. Branches grow from the pith at the center of the tree, deflecting the grain, and appear as knots when the board is radially cut.

Also, the grain of some woods is naturally larger than others; ash, for example, despite flat and unbroken fibers would require filling with composition to achieve a smooth surface (see page 100).

END GRAIN

Reference should also be made here to the term "end grain." End grain refers to the opened tracheid vessels caused when a horizontal cut is made across the log, i.e., a cut perpendicular to the direction of the grain. As we shall see in Chapter 9, end grain wood behaves differently from regular grain (approached parallel to the grain) and consequently involves special treatment on the part of the cabinetmaker.

WOOD FIGURE

Figure is the natural design or pattern seen on the surface of a given cut board or wood surface. This pattern should not be confused with the grain of the wood. Figure is brought out by cutting timbers so that veneers or solid surfaces display various kinds of irregularities in the grain, variations in color, and other internal effects. The manner in which the log is cut can be tangential, plain, radial, or quarter sawed. (See illustration 21.) There are many kinds and examples of figure.

CROTCHWOOD FIGURE

This figure, especially examples in mahogany, is probably one of the most dramatic and universally exploited types of figure for veneer. It is formed below the point where a tree trunk forks into two large branches resulting from distortions in the elements of growth. It is apparent in the figuring of tangentially-cut veneers. The spreading direction of the elements appears as inverted arcs forming what is known as swirl crotch figure. When the veneer cuts reach the point of the crotch, where the greatest stress and compression has occurred, a feather figure or plume-like formation penetrates or divides the swirl figure. It is interesting to note that

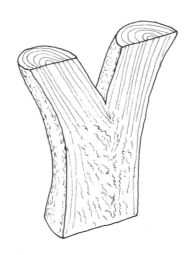

11. Bisected wood crotch showing disturbed wood grain at the fork.

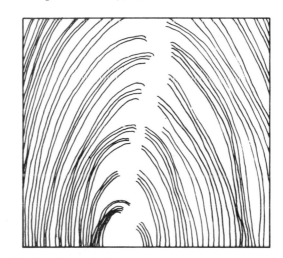

12. Swirl crotch figure

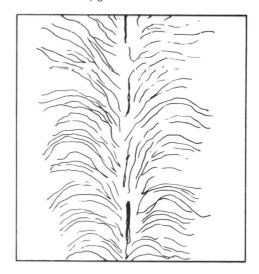

13. Feather or plume figure

feather or swirl crotch veneers were usually laid upon vertical surfaces with the grain running in the opposite direction to that which it takes in the tree.

FIDDLE-BACK FIGURE

Fiddle-back derives from wavy grain. The markings, resembling ripples, are brought out by cutting through the crests of successive undulations in the grain, and they are

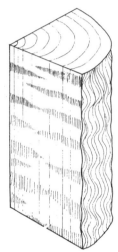

14. Fiddle-back figure as seen in a radially-cut log.

best shown when the surface has been cut radially from the source. Mahogany, maple and sycamore trees are likely timbers for this figure.

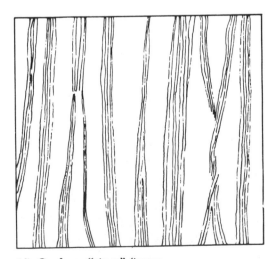

15. Curly or "tiger" figure

CURLY FIGURE

Especially associated with so-called tiger maple, curly figure is also derived from the irregularities of the wood elements at the bases of large branches. It is displayed in wavy line markings and sometimes curls. However, these horizontal figures are less delicate and more erratic than fiddle-back patterns. Curly figure can be seen on the drawer fronts of the highboy shown in illustration 193, page 154.

OYSTER FIGURE

This figure comes from circular or elliptical patterns displayed by the concentric

16. Oyster figure

growth rings in thin cross sections, or diagonally-cut sections of branches. These sections are known as oyster pieces and parquetry panels of oyster veneer on table surfaces and cabinet doors were very fashionable in 17th century England.

BURL FIGURE

The veneers sliced from burls—excrescences found growing on the trunks of various trees—contain tiny knot-like markings or eyes. A curly grain and thus figure appears, often forming loops around the knotty eyes. The burl veneers of walnut are the best

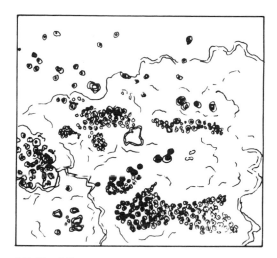

17. Burl figure

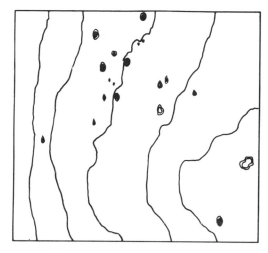

19. Birds-eye figure

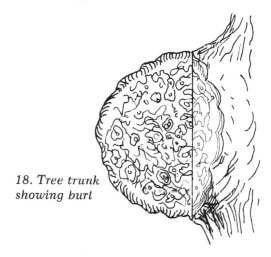

18. Tree trunk
showing burl

GROWTH-RING FIGURE

Perhaps the most obvious and basic figure, this is produced in plain-sawed wood cut through the annual layers (or rings) of timbers. The marked differences which occur in the wood substance developed during the early and late periods of each growing season appear as stripes, parabolas, and ellipses. Oak, chestnut, ash and elm have very conspicuous markings of this type. Examples of growth-ring figure appear in illustrations 10 and 22.

known for furniture use. Notice the Queen Anne dressing table top shown in illustration 138, page 106.

BIRDS-EYE FIGURE

Bird's-eye figure is apparently caused by a fungus that attacks some North American and European maple trees resulting in brownish specks which extend through several layers of growth rings. The wood is tangentially-sawed, bringing out the figure by cutting through the specks which are found in irregular or circular, almost crater-like markings.

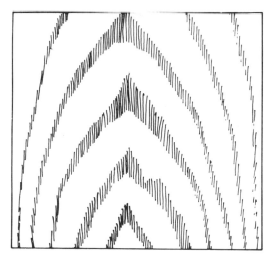

20. Parabola growth ring figure

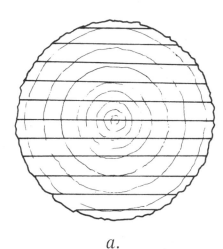

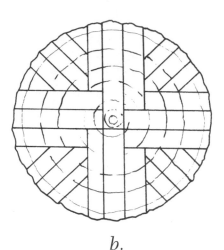

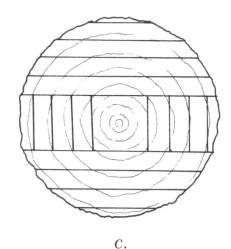

a.   *b.*   *c.*

21. Wood Conversion Into Boards

a. Plain Sawn Log. Boards cut at edge, most tangential, have straight growth-ring figure; those cut through the heart have full growth-ring figure.

b. Quarter or Radial Cut Log. All boards have full figure, are less liable to warp, and are stronger.

c. Tangential cut log or Boxed Heart Log. No part of the heart appears on any board.

d. End section of plain sawn log

e. End section of quartered board

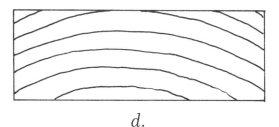

d.

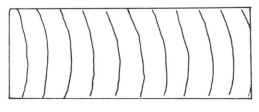

e.

CUTTING OF THE WOOD

Regardless of furniture style and type or kind of wood used, it has always been necessary to begin by cutting logs into boards. (Consider some of the conversions here illus- trated.) Due to the plentiful wood supply, only the largest trees were felled in the early eighteenth century, thereby providing wonderfully wide boards for use in furniture making. Some of the largest eighteenth-century tea table tops measure 31″ and 35″ in diameter, the top all one board.) When narrow planks —18″ or less—are detected in an early piece, it is an indication of the use of wood of later introduction. (See gateleg table, illustration

199, page 16.) Tools for cutting were simple and signs of their use remain in evidence on a finished piece of furniture—an excellent guide for establishing authenticity.

THE PIT SAW

The early pit saw was not conducive to producing lumber of perfect "standard size," although it was amazingly accurate. The boards will vary slightly in width and thickness, despite a cabinetmaker's efforts to minimize these differences by planing and sawing.

If eighteenth-century boards are measured they will show discrepancies in size.

SAW KERF MARKS

The saw marks made by the blade of the pit saw, known as saw kerf marks, are long, straight, parallel marks. When the totally manual pit saw was replaced by the man- or water-powered rip saw in the middle of the eighteenth century, the saw kerf marks remained straight, parallel, and relatively regular.

A Sawyer.

22. *Cutting Timber With The Pit Saw.* (*Engraving,* The Book of English Trades and Library of the Useful Arts, *London, 1827.*) *The man at the top controlled the line of the two-handed saw and was called the top sawyer; the man in the pit merely supplied energy. Photograph courtesy the American Antiquarian Society.*

23. *Backside of 17th century desk box showing straight parallel kerf marks.*

24. Mr. Smart's circular saw mill with continuous rotary blade cutting appeared in print as early as 1816 in A New and Complete Dictionary of Arts and Sciences Including the Latest Improvement and Discovery and the Present State of Every Branch of Human Knowledge by George Gregory. (Isaac Pierce, Philadelphia, 1816.) Photograph courtesy the American Antiquarian Society.

THE STEAM-DRIVEN CIRCULAR SAW

This saw, part of the change brought by the Industrial Revolution, made its appearance about 1820. A mechanized means of sawing logs using the rotary blade with cutting therefore continuous, it produced a widely curving or circular kerf mark. From 1820 onwards, power-driven circular blades have been used for reducing logs to lumber and for other refinements, hence the simple but important conclusion that a piece of furniture showing circular kerf marks on its

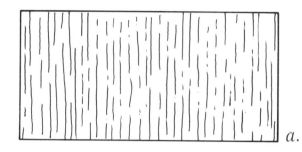
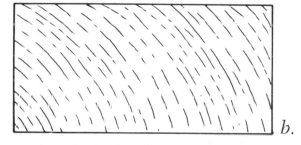

25. *Saw Kerf Marks*

    a. *Straight kerf marks*
    b. *Curving kerf marks*

inside or secondary surfaces (surfaces which have not received final dressing), must have been constructed after the year 1820. Note these marks on the photographed Victorian desk drawer bottom (illustration 26).

An eighteenth-century piece of furniture conversely should show signs of straight kerf marks. For example, straight kerf marks may be found on the back, on the inside and on the underside of a veneered walnut Queen Anne period highboy. This evidence should remain on at least one of the above-mentioned surfaces to support authenticity, although

many times surfaces were planed smooth. If there are no straight marks, or circular marks are found instead (often the ridges can be felt when they cannot be seen) the piece must be questioned; the available kerf mark evidence certainly does not agree with the constructional detail appropriate to a piece of that period.

26. *Mid-19th century desk drawer bottom showing circular saw marks.*

TURNING OF THE WOOD

The skill of turning (or cutting) on a lathe is a fascinating and ancient craft. (Turning is the practice of shaping objects by means of stationary cutting tools brought into contact with objects held and rotated rapidly on a lathe.) Thus, the final turned shape must be contained within the square section of wood from which it was worked. Lathes date back to at least the seventeenth century and have been used in some capacity despite fashion changes ever since. Like the saw, lathes have been mechanized until turning is an automatic operation today, but during the seventeenth and eighteenth centuries, successful turning was literally in the hands of the "turner." Therefore, each of the turned legs and spindles of a piece of early furniture will be unique—no two turned legs will measure exactly the same, using a callipers, for although the legs were turned from "patterns," their final shape is the turner's deed.

27. *The turner at his lathe as pictured in* The Book of English Trades, *1807. "The thing to be turned is fixed on the lengthened axis of the smaller wheel, and upon the prop or rest, the chisel or other cutting instrument is supported; and being brought to touch the wood while it is swiftly turning round, it takes off shavings to the greatest nicety." Photograph courtesy the American Antiquarian Society.*

Turner.

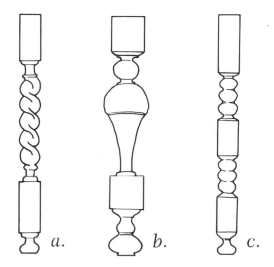

28. *Characteristic turned legs from the late 17th century:*

 a. twist-turned
 b. trumpet-turned
 c. baluster-turned

The obvious conclusion is thus that if the six "trumpet" turned legs of a supposed seventeenth century William and Mary highboy measure exactly the same in size and detail, they cannot have been turned by hand—the only possible means in the seventeenth and eighteenth centuries. A special form of turning, twist turning, so popular in the seventeenth century was a combination of plain turning, carving, rasp and file work, plus scraping, and should consequently also prove inconsistent when measured.

PREPARING THE WOOD

DRESSING MARKS

 The woodworker or cabinetmaker used many tools and made great efforts to ready his sawn pieces of timber for furniture construction. While examining secondary wood surfaces for saw kerf marks, one should be aware of the slight ridges and hollows made by the blade of the smoothing plane, called dressing marks or hand-planing marks. These can be both seen and felt and indicate the extent to which the early cabinetmaker attempted to plane smooth his wood in areas which were not going to be seen. The primary surfaces were carefully smoothed, sanded and finished with shellac, varnish or paint, etc.; the top and front generally receiving the cabinetmaker's greatest attention and effort. In contrast, many areas of primary surface with small visibility received relatively little attention: remote moldings, backsides of legs, concave surfaces of trumpet legs, etc. Note the backside of the pictured sofa leg (illustration 32) attributed to the renowned cabinetmaker Duncan Phyfe.

 Of interest is the fact that there will usually be a pattern or rhythm to the marks (four grooves one time, four grooves in-between the next time, for example); the pattern will vary from man to man and from tool to tool, but it will be there. These marks were primarily made with planes and various scraping, abrading, and paring tools well into the

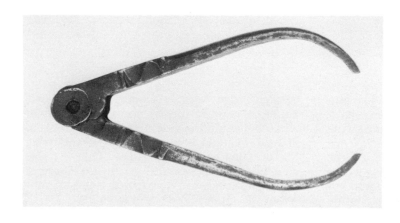

29. *Pair of callipers circa 1750–1775. This tool was used repeatedly by the wood turner to check the diameter or thickness of stock being turned on a lathe. Photograph courtesy the Henry Francis du Pont Winterthur Museum.*

30. 18th century Compass Plane with a convex sole particularly useful for smoothing curved parts of furniture. Photograph courtesy the Henry Francis du Pont Winterthur Museum.

32. Backside of a reeded sofa leg, a primary surface left incomplete (without reeding) due to little visibility.

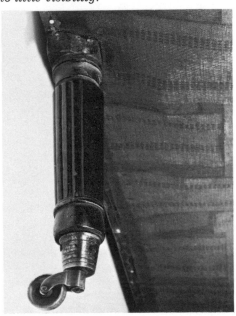

31. Backside of a high chest or highboy showing dressing marks left on secondary surfaces.

1800's when mass-production methods outmoded such handwork. Thus, furniture showing these marks is likely to have been made prior to 1800.

A test and method of demonstrating the presence of dressing marks in cases where these marks are neither apparent to the naked eye nor easily felt with the finger tips, is the straight edge test. By placing a rule (ruler) on top of a wood surface and spotting a light directly behind the rule, light will shine from the grooves and hollows thereby dramatizing the dressing mark undulations. This test also demonstrates the natural grain differences of spring and summer tree growth—one shrinks more and thus is lower than the other.

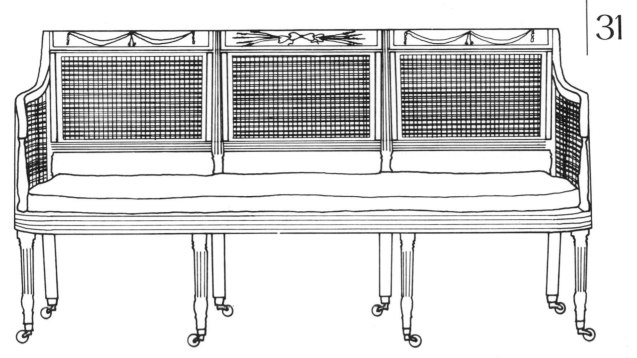

33. *Early 19th century Duncan Phyfe style sofa (see leg detail, illustration 32).*

34. *Underside of 18th century drawer showing the rhythmic hand planing marks and the bevelled edge for easier joining of the bottom into the side rebate.*

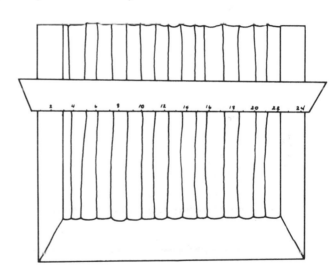

35. *Straight-edge test.*

SMOOTHING AND CUTTING TOOLS

The careful smoothing of primary surfaces was done with an assortment of planes, scrapers and sandpaper. A perfectly smooth, unblemished surface was always the goal, despite its impossibility. The simple fact that surfaces were being worked by hand implied human imperfections. Thus, the hand pressure applied by even the master craftsman on his tools would vary from movement to movement. Furthermore, some spots on the wood were softer or harder and required additional pressure. Too much pressure could be inadvertently applied causing a slight hollow. These slight undulations or waves indicate to us that a surface was planed (or dressed) by hand—which was the necessary state of affairs for woodworkers in the sixteenth, seventeenth and eighteenth centuries.

Modern machine-made pieces *have* been known to have been hand-planed with old tools to emulate true antiques and have thus been mistaken by some as being old. Other construction detail will quickly destroy this illusion. Then too, genuine old pieces sometimes suffer the unhappy fate of being refinished by an amateur refinisher. His inadequate efforts, mistakes, and in some cases "butchery," should never be mistaken for the hand-craft of the early cabinetmaker.

Sandpapering was an important process in the final preparation of primary wood surfaces before a finish was applied. Sandpaper was valued and used by craftsmen in some form long before machine-coated modern cloths and papers were introduced in 1872. Prior to 1800, woodworkers and cabinetmakers used dried shark skin for smoothing wood. It had strong and long-lasting abrasive action with a great undercut, meaning it only cut in one direction. Abrasive papers and cloths were invented about 1800 and then they were made by hand, with resulting variations in the evenness of the coating.

MOLDING PLANES, GOUGES AND SCRATCH STOCKS

Real appreciation of undulating hand-planing marks comes when we examine the moldings made by hand with molding planes. For example, let us consider the ogee (S-shaped) molding of the panel frames belonging to a Chippendale style secretary door. By standing as close as possible to such a molding and "sighting down" (or up), one quickly sees the unevenness of the planing. Hand-planed marks become apparent when any molding is sighted in this way—door frames, chimney moldings, or the cornice moldings at the top of a secretary or highboy. Sight a modern machine-made molding and note how perfectly even it is by comparison.

36. English mid-18th century tea table top with subtle reflecting surface undulations, evidence that the surface has been hand dressed.

This sighting test or exercise can also be used for other molded and cut surfaces to determine whether planing and cutting has been done by hand. The reeded posts of a Sheraton-style canopy bed, for example, can be sighted up and down to ascertain hand craftsmanship—hand cutting by gouges and/or a scratch stock will appear in the form of visible undulations. Note the photographed round reeded projecting leg of a Sheraton-style sideboard and the unevenness of the reeding when this detail is sighted (illustration 37). Early inlay work can also be sighted; its unevenness is due to the use of these same early hand tools.

Another interesting test is to take a wax impression of one section of the molding and then compare this with other sections of the molding. If the molding was really planed by hand, the impression will not match up perfectly anywhere and will vary with every inch. If the impression does match uniformly along the molding, it is reasonable to believe that it has been made by modern methods or at least machine sanded or dressed in our time.

37. *Sighting down a leg to ascertain hand craftsmanship.*

MARKING TOOLS

The marking tools and gauges, vital to the furniture maker in the days of total hand craftsmanship and which have since been replaced by modern, fast and perhaps more accurate methods, have left their signs on the furniture which required their use. When the important function of these tools is understood, remaining evidence of their work becomes a valuable aid in dating a piece of furniture as being very old—1830 or earlier. The awl, which resembles a modern ice pick, was used in place of today's pencil for marking all sorts of measurements needed in the construction process. The resulting scored marks or lines will be found at many points and can be quickly identified when one thinks through the construction process to the measurement or mark likely to have been re-

38. *Sheraton-style sideboard of mahogany and satinwood made in 1808–1809 in Salem, Massachusetts, by William Hook. (See detail of leg, illustration 37.)*

quired at that spot. For example, in examining the dovetails found on the side of a drawer, almost invariably one will find a scored gauge line (groove, mark, etc.) struck at the edge of the dovetails. This was simply the line marking the inside edge of the dovetail cut-

back chair (illustration 144, page 115) and on the Pilgrim chair (illustration 170, page 135). These marks were made with the blade of a chisel when the parts were turned as guides for places where holes were to be bored for cross stretchers, or where mortises were

39. *The scratch or scribe awl with its thin round shank of iron tapering to a sharp point, was used to mark the surface of the wood with guide lines. The tool was also useful in making starting holes for the flat-ended screws in use during the 18th and early 19th centuries. This awl, 4" long and dating between 1820 and 1850, was used in the Dominy Woodworking Shop, East Hampton, Long Island. Photograph courtesy the Henry Francis du Pont Winterthur Museum.*

ting. In the drawer photograph (illustration 46, page 43), the scored line can be seen, marking the dovetails. Measurement marks can also be found near a mortise and tenon joint made by the mortise gauge to indicate where the mortise was to be cut out.

If one studies the front legs and back uprights of old Windsor chairs and slat-back chairs made of turned parts, faint score lines or marks can be seen. Examples can be recognized in the photograph of the child's slat-

to be cut for the back slats. Such scored lines are good indications of age. Of further note is the staggering of these scored stretchers to prevent too much wood being cut from one point, a good precaution which was abandoned at a later date. Incidentally, because so many Windsor chairs were carefully stripped of their paint in the 1920's, alas the fashion then, traces of original paint can sometimes be found in the scored lines—or when a member becomes loose at the joint.

2

THE CABINETMAKER AND SOME OF HIS CONSTRUCTION CONSIDERATIONS

CABINETMAKER IS A HALLOWED word today. We stand in awe of his sense of design, proportion and detail and his skillful abilities to execute his plan, as we behold his product now many years old. One can quickly become absorbed in a study of individual cabinetmakers and their characteristic work. Regionalism and local schools of cabinetmakers can be explored and compared. Published books and catalogs prepared by cabinetmakers—including a 1775 Philadelphia version of Chippendale's Director which was attempted but, unfortunately, never produced by cabinetmaker John Folwell—are fascinating. It should be remembered, that the cabinetmaker was a simple craftsman. Some were better than others, but none imagined himself to be a great artist. Depending on how a given customer weighed the various cabinetmaking decisions—choice of wood, amount and quality of detail, kind and amount of finish, etc.—all affecting time and price—the completed piece was or was not representative of the cabinetmaker's skill. It should also be kept in mind that there are careless workers in any field and all cabinetmakers did not constantly try to do their best. It is important to keep our image of the cabinetmaker, famous or not, in proper perspective.

For the most part, woodworkers, joiners and cabinetmakers did good work and took pride in doing the best possible job within the definition of the project. At times they were most ingenious and showed a true eye for beauty, but all the while they were basically doing the job for which they had been trained by the apprentice system. In contemporary terms, they were concerned with paying the grocery bill or having the funds available for the purchase of a new vehicle. This meant that the individual craftsman moved along quickly with his projects, and hoped Mrs. Jones would pay him promptly. (If she did not he might eliminate a coat of shellac next time, especially if he was in a hurry.) How surprised, amused and pleased cabinetmakers of the eighteenth century, for example, would be were they to learn how they are revered today.

CHOOSING THE WOOD

Like all businessmen (Thomas Chippendale has been described as the first successful interior decorator), cabinetmakers had many practical decisions to make with regard to each piece of furniture. Wood considerations, including the choice of wood, were critical. Soft woods, cheap and available, were utilized in areas not seen and where strength was not necessary, such as drawer interiors. Costly hardwoods were used to provide strength and for their handsome appearance in parts that were seen.

The pierced and carved splat of a Chippendale style chair, so inherently weak by design, required a hard, strong wood to resist the pressure of a seated person's back. Bed rails and chair legs both required strong woods to do their jobs of supporting much weight. Indeed, without the popularity and ability of walnut, cherry and mahogany—all hardwoods—to support the weight of a chest of drawers (filled) on tall slender legs, the highboy could not exist. The cabinetmaker's sophisticated craftsmanship showing his control of the strain put upon his chosen wood and its ability to withstand this pressure, can be seen in the carved ball-and-claw foot of a Goddard-Townsend mahogany high chest of drawers or highboy. So strong is the wood that the talons have been undercut and the great weight of the piece rests on a much reduced area.

The quality of the kind of wood selected was also a consideration. Knots, for example, were an unwelcome flaw and weakness in all wood. They often would fall out and while present play havoc with any applied finish. Fortunately, it was possible to obtain wood without this imperfection and this was done whenever possible.

Cabinetmakers have always selected their woods carefully for the purposes planned. In addition to quality and strength of the chosen wood, its color and indeed the beauty and interest of the grain's figure were important. Duncan Phyfe, working in New York between 1795 and 1847, so loved and admired figured mahogany that he eliminated most ornament and detail to allow the wood to show its full glory.

Cabinetmakers and patrons alike have admired the beauty of exciting wood figure. To work up patterns for matched drawer and door fronts and to utilize the interesting fig-

ure of woods whose source is an unusual circumstance and whose future movement is unpredictable (burls and whorls), is a challenge to the veneering skill of the cabinetmaker. Veneering also conserves highly figured wood.

The cabinetmaker accomplished his goals and produced the superb products which are so loved and admired today through great understanding—indeed, scientific knowledge in part—of his basic material—wood. Some of this understanding came from trial and error experience; some came from lessons learned while serving as an apprentice or working in a joiner or cabinetmaking shop, and some came from an innate love and interest in the material. There are few crafts in which one works with a material that is in a perfectly natural state. Most substances are purified or manufactured, whereas wood comes to the plane and chisel just as it grew in the forest.

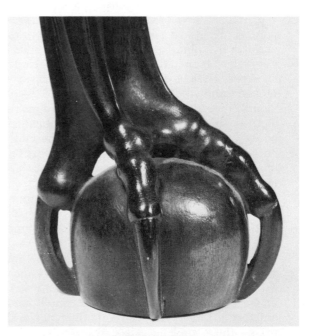

40. *Carved ball-and-claw foot circa 1760–1780, Newport. The Goddard-Townsend families of cabinetmakers were unique in their abilities to undercut the talons on their ball-and-claw feet. This superb example has not only the sides of the ball free, but it is possible to run a thread over the top of the ball.*

WOOD MOVEMENT

The knowledge and understanding developed by the furniture maker placed him on guard for some of the problems posed by wood. Wood movement was a serious concern, in the stages of construction and after the piece of furniture was completed. Since wood shrinks and swells, seasonally and daily, due to changes in the moisture content of the atmosphere, seasoning newly cut timber was an important first step in stabilizing the moisture content of the wood. The movement would not be so great thereafter. Various finishes applied to wood surfaces also kept movement to a minimum.

Details and kinds of construction were sometimes adopted to allow for this. Panel and frame construction was a clever way of overcoming difficulties caused by such movement (see Chapter 4). As the panel expanded with additional moisture absorption it filled the leeway space in the grooved frame. Illustration 41 shows this kind of construction where the frame has come partly away. As the panel shrank with reduced moisture, it was free to contract away from the frame and thus not split from being held in place. Again as a reaction to wood movement, cabinetmakers often extended the length of a drawer bottom beyond its frame at the back, thereby assuring a complete drawer bottom panel were shrinkage to reduce its size.

The understanding of wood movement was sometimes used to advantage. The effectiveness of old cornerblocks suggests this. A very common example is the corner block of a bracket foot. The grain of the triangular corner block is vertical, while that of the foot itself is horizontal. The tendency is for the foot to shrink and become lower in winter and swell slightly in summer while the block remains the same height (its shrinkage is horizontal), thus performing its function of support. (This movement will in time cause the glue to give way.) Another example would be the triangular horizontal-grain corner block found supporting the legs of a mid-18th

41. 17th century oak front chest panel of frame and panel construction. Note how the panel is recessed into the lower rail.

century Massachusetts chair. Again, the tensions complement each other.

Many of the cabinetmaker's techniques and uses of wood depended on minimum wood movement; sometimes this gamble was successful, and sometimes tell-tale signs and shrinkage problems were the result. There were times, as well, when fashion and novelty seem to have over-ruled wisdom in choice of construction material and method. Again it must be considered that the furniture-maker through history has always been engaged in trade.

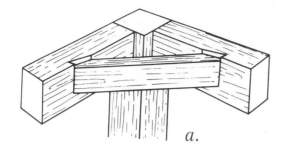

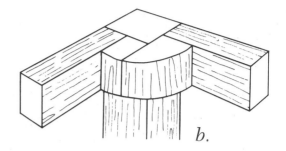

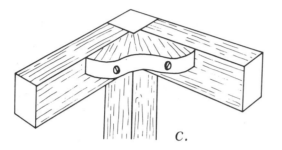

42. *Corner blocks.*

a. Open strut corner block
b. Solid two-piece quarter-round corner block attached with glue.
c. One-piece bracket or triangular-shaped corner block attached with glue and nails or screws.

Many tricks of the trade learned and adopted by the furniture-maker bear witness to his knowledge, sensitivity and sensibility towards his craft. Awareness of wood's tendency to split along its grain meant that the individual nails or screws in a row would be slightly staggered so as not to crack the board. Another device was to position the stretchers of a Windsor chair at different levels to obtain maximum support. The appropriate choice of joint for a given purpose was another important decision, and one made well most of the time judging from the number of untouched old joints still doing their intended jobs today.

There is much question as to the cabinet-maker's awareness and consideration for the effect of patina—the soft mellow surface look achieved by a combination of factors over time. He may have admired the patina surface of old furniture in his time, though there is little reference or evidence of this. He certainly admired the wood with which he worked and was eager to preserve and enhance its beauty with the best possible finish. His longer-range concern, I think, was preservation. The subtle changes and effects we call patina today can be considered a modern pleasure and a special bonus—the result of the cabinetmaker's skill but not directly attributable to it. We were not there, however, and thus will never know for certain.

3

JOININGS

DISCOVERING HOW AND WHERE the parts of a piece of furniture are joined together has all the fascination of a jigsaw puzzle. Locating the joinings can be a real challenge, especially in cases where they have been well disguised. (French ébénistes or cabinetmakers were particularly skilled at concealing their joined areas.) The decisions as to where to join the parts of a piece were important, as the end result had not only to work well structurally and withstand stress and strain given the function of the piece, but to be aesthetically pleasing as well. (See illustration 43 to see how certain chairs, tables and chests have been joined.)

To aid the cabinetmaker with his joining task were a variety of joints he could employ, as well as hardware (nails and screws) and adhesives, i.e., glue, to reinforce his choice. Of the many joints known and used by early furniture makers, each had its own characteristics, functions and best uses. The cabinetmaker understood this well, judging from what we observe in old pieces. Not only did he use the most effective joint for a particular joining, but he worked out the correct proportions to hold the piece firmly together right up to today. He clearly took great pride in the craftsmanship necessary to make a joint which fitted together and worked perfectly. One of the joys in exploring old joints is the sense it gives of the cabinetmaker's pride and skill. Another joy is the variety of joints and the variations on any given type that one finds when one takes the time to look closely and to understand.

JOINTS

DOVETAIL JOINT

The dovetail joint is one of the oldest and most successful joints in furniture making history. Whether hand- or even machine-cut, it is still the best method of joining two pieces of wood together in their width at right angles to each other. At a typical auction, showing, or antique shop, one will often see people pulling out the drawers of case pieces and seemingly studying or admiring the dovetails—so-called because one part is tapered in shape rather like a dove's tail and fits into a corresponding recess. By its shape it thus resists any outward pull. The dovetail joint is a challenge to the talents of all cabinetmakers. Hand-made dovetails, with their subtle irregularities and variety of sizes can be easily spotted as such in comparison with the regular, rather short and stubby machine-made dovetails—a good first indication that the piece in question is indeed old and hand-made. A scored line will also be visible, marking the gauge line of hand-cut dovetails.

43. Furniture joinings.

Cabinetmakers have a traditional rule for dovetail measurements. All dovetails are made on variations of the proportions of 3″ up (in the vise) and ⅝″ across. (See illustration 45.) These proportions apply regardless of the length or the number of dovetails planned. The best angle for the dovetail is about 12 degrees. If the slope or pitch is made steeper, the corners will tend to break off; if made shallower, the dovetail will be weak.

Dovetails found on early sixteenth and seventeenth century drawers tend to be large

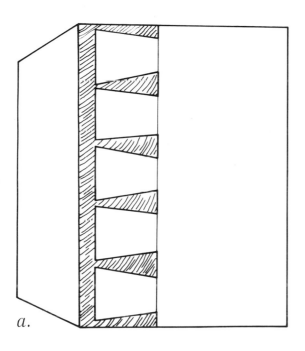

a.

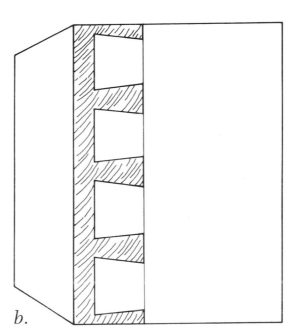

b.

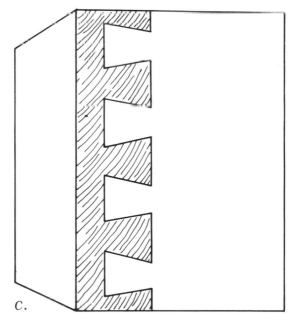

c.

44. Kinds of Dovetails

a. Fine Hand-cut Single-lapped Dovetail Joining. This joint is used for drawers, etc., where one face must not show the joint and the dovetails are thus set back by a small lap. The angle or slope of the dovetail constitutes its holding power against lateral strain.

b. Hand-cut Single-lapped Dovetail Joining. The slopes of the dovetail sides usually vary slightly since the cabinetmaker generally cuts them out freehand without using a bevel.

c. Machine-cut Single-lapped Dovetail Joining. The tails and recesses are uniform and exactly the same size. No gauge line is necessary.

and rough; nevertheless they serve their constructional purpose very well. The dovetail became more refined during the eighteenth century and directly reflected the skill of the individual cabinetmaker. Country cabinetmakers tended to make straightforward, husky dovetails with few in number per drawer side, thereby taking minimum risk of mishap during the cutting process. In contrast, when one finds carefully cut, geometrically correct dovetails with many per drawer side, one knows the piece to be the work of a master craftsman. Put another way, without so much as opening the drawer of a beautiful eighteenth century Philadelphia dressing table, one might well expect to find very fine dovetails.

Machine-cut dovetailing, often with eight or more small dovetails per drawer side, was introduced during the nineteenth century. Machine-cut dovetails are easy to identify, being evenly spaced, symmetrical and uniform. (The spaces between the dovetails will often prove the counterpart of the dovetail in size and shape.) Some Victorian dovetailing was made with scallops and pegs, again positive indication of the piece's nineteenth century origin.

There are many variations of the handmade dovetail joint. We will limit ourselves here to a brief descriptive summary for purposes of recognition, since more detailed information is available in any woodworking book or dictionary.

46. Hand-cut drawer dovetails. The dovetails ▶ *are wider than the pins or recesses (which run almost to a point), and the dovetail slopes vary slightly one from the next. Note vertical scored line at the root of the drawer dovetails serving as a guideline for consistent dovetail length.*

The single-lapped dovetail is a joint used commonly in core, box and drawer construction, in which one part, usually with the pins, has a lap or covering piece so that the ends of the dovetails are concealed (see illustration 44). Its particular value is in core work in which the joint does not show on one face. (When veneer is anticipated for drawer parts, the lapped dovetail also eliminates possible veneer adhering problems due to through-dovetail end grain.) The double-lapped or secret-lapped dovetail is a dovetail joint in which both joining pieces have a lap. The lap in one piece is allowed to project. Thus, the only indication of the presence of the joint is the thin line of end grain. This joint is often used for the tops of bureaux and cabinets.

Slot (slip) dovetails are cut in the width rather than the thickness of the wood and are used in plinths, cornices, etc. This is a heavy duty joint, and illustration 51 shows how it was used to anchor the four legs into the pedestal of an Empire card table. Note how the veneer damage of the secretary-

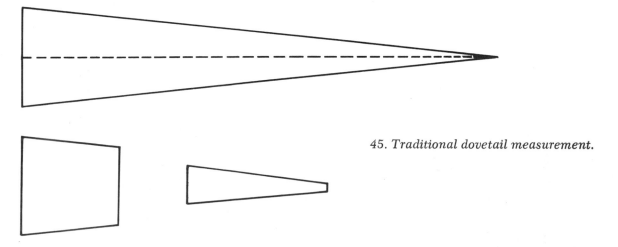

45. Traditional dovetail measurement.

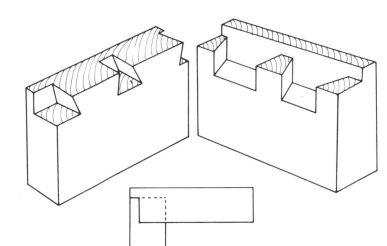

49. Secret (double lap) dovetail joint. The dovetails are set back by a small lap on both faces of the joint.

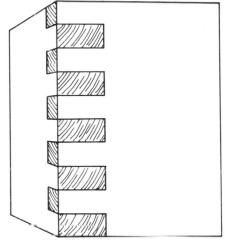

47. Machine-cut square through dovetail with tails and pins of equal size.

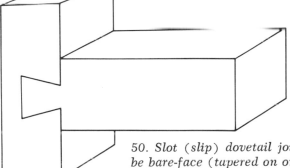

50. Slot (slip) dovetail joint. This joint can be bare-face (tapered on one face only), double-tapered (as shown), or stopped (this the most laborious as it cannot be sawn through but must be chopped out and hence is only used where the actual joints must be hidden on one face).

48. Late 19th century pine drawer with mechanical scallop and peg dovetail-type joining. The drawer side was scalloped to fit into the drawer front matching scallops and over the drawer front side protruding "pegs or pins."

51. Underside of pedestal base, Empire card ▶ table. The four legs are slot dovetailed into the pedestal base and the pedestal base is joined to the pedestal in the center with a reinforced (wedged) through-tenon mortise and tenon joint.

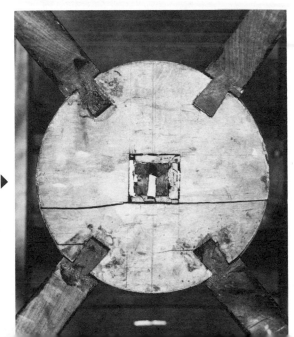

bookcase (illustration 139, page 107) exposes a drawer support type slot dovetail. (This is also called a dovetail housing joint.)

The mitre dovetail (or secret mitre) is a corner joint in which the dovetail is entirely concealed. This joint is used chiefly for outside joints, plinths and work in which it is desirable to hide the joint. The Chinese considered mitring the most beautiful form of jointing parts of furniture and used the mitre

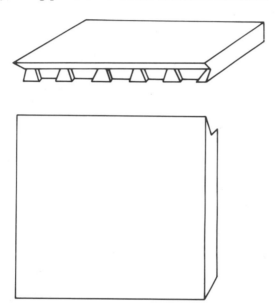

52. Mitre Dovetail Joint. The mitre or secret mitre dovetail.

mortise and tenon and mitre dovetail joints extensively, along with panel and frame construction. In fact, the mitred dovetail was so refined by the Chinese cabinetmaker that the dovetails are completely hidden on both sides. (See the Chinese chair seat, illustration 6, page 13.)

MORTISE AND TENON JOINT

The strongest, perhaps oldest, and most versatile of all joints is the mortise and tenon (see illustration 3). This joint is such that one piece has a projection (the tenon) which fits into a corresponding recess (the mortise) chiseled out of the other piece. Used most successfully as the major joint in chair construction, this is an important joint in table

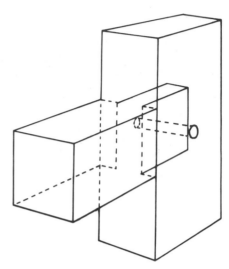

53. Mortise and Tenon Joint

construction as well, particularly in the form of the bridle joint which joins the legs to the table. The mortise and tenon joint is also used for all kinds of framing. It is used for connecting the rails and headboard of a bed and for uniting the four sides of a case piece. Sometimes this joint is pegged to provide even greater strength, and these pegs will always be visible. Other variations of the mortise and tenon joint include the hauch tenon, the through tenon, the blind tenon and the wedge tenon. (An example of a wedge tenon can be seen in illustration 51, where it is used to anchor the pedestal to the base platform of the table.)

The draw-bore-pin joint is a form of mortise and tenon joint of great strength and tightness. Because of its power, this joint is used in massive structure joinery—a bed rail for a heavy bedpost, for example. Through a special technique, the mortise and tenon joint is locked and the tenon is forced home into its mortise. This is done by passing a peg or pin through staggered holes in both parts of the joint, thereby exerting pressure on the joint. That is to say, a hole is bored right through the mortised piece, the tenon put in position, and the bit pressed into the hole so that it marks the tenon. The tenon is then withdrawn and its hole bored slightly nearer the shoulder. A draw-bore-pin (a tapered rod)

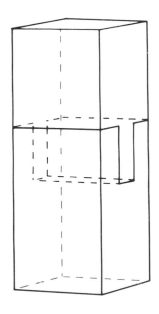

54. *The bridle joint, sometimes referred to as a "slot" mortise and tenon joint, is marked out with a mortise gauge, which is worked from the face sides and set to give a slot about ⅓ the total thickness with equal wood left on either side.*

55. *The bridle joint here forms a strong connection between the back leg of the wing chair and the back frame support. (See illustration 94, page 74, for an over-all photograph of this stripped barrel-back wing chair.)*

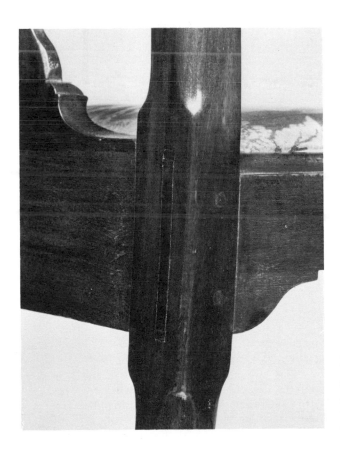

56. *Through-tenon mortise and tenon joint. The tenon extends through the chair stile, thereby showing end grain on the rear edge of the stile. The joint is frequently found in Chippendale-style rococo Philadelphia chairs of the mid-18th century.*

is then knocked into the hole, forcing the two off-center holes to meet. The pin is then withdrawn and a wooden peg is inserted.

MITRE JOINT

The common mitre joint has always been considered an important and useful joint by cabinetmakers and is one easily recognized by students. It is formed by the intersection of two moldings or two plain pieces of wood.

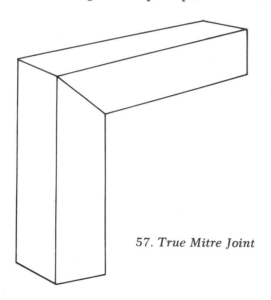

57. True Mitre Joint

The angle at which the molding is cut should halve the overall angle of the joining pieces, and since most moldings join at right-angles, the mitring angle is 45 degrees. (A simple example would be the mitred corners of a picture frame.) On occasion a curved molding joins a straight molding of the same section, thus the mitre joint must be curved. By locating and studying mitre joints, students of furniture can ascertain whether they were properly made for their time and whether or not they have been tampered with since. This is helpful for dating purposes. The same reasoning, of course, can be applied to all traditional old joints.

RULE JOINT

To those with mechanical minds, the rule joint provides special appeal. It is at its most fascinating and attractive when used for its main purpose, the leaves of a drop-leaf table. (Note the rule joint on the drop-leaf table, illustration 160, page 127.) The idea of the rule joint is that where the extension leaf hangs down, the ovolo (half-round) edge is seen. This becomes invisible when the leaf is raised. The rule joint derives its name from its approximation to the brass joint of the cabinetmaker's rule and its use dates back to the early 1700's. This type of joint is still used today, there being little difference between the old and modern joints except that in some of the old ones the curved lip of the joint is noticeably less than half the thickness of the table top. Unfortunately, however, this joint is inherently weak. It cracks easily and is difficult to repair, especially when the trouble is combined with hinge problems.

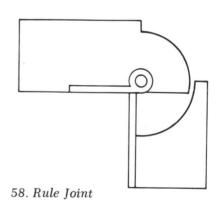

58. Rule Joint

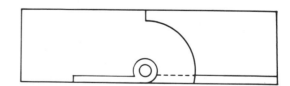

KNUCKLE JOINT

The knuckle joint is related to the rule joint in design and purpose. Swing legs for card and occasional tables are hinged to the underframing of the table with this type of joining.

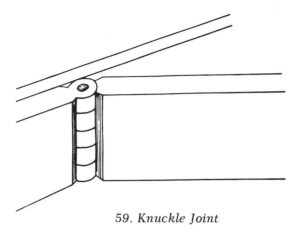

59. *Knuckle Joint*

DOWELLED JOINT

One of the less skillful means of joining two pieces of wood is with wooden dowels. A dowel is a round wooden peg, and any form of joint in which dowels are used to hold parts together is called a dowelled joint. The dowel is glued into holes bored into the two pieces to be joined. Dowels in a variety of materials have been used for a variety of purposes since ancient times but dowelled joints tend to appear in less important late nineteenth and early twentieth century work to replace the mortise and tenon. Dowelled joints provide a cheap and quick method of joinery but are comparatively weak—any strain on the joint or shrinkage in the surrounding wood is likely to cause the joint to fail. Examples of eighteenth century furniture with dowelled joints are unknown. (This joint should not be confused with the pegged joint in which a wooden pin is passed through a mortise and tenon to hold the two firmly together.)

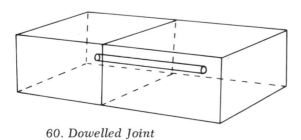

60. *Dowelled Joint*

PEGS

Pegs alone have been used in some form from the beginning of furniture making and continue to be an important construction material today. Used to fasten parts together, wooden pegs (or pins) were easy to make— in whatever size or shape needed to do the job—and they were much cheaper than nails. Early glues were not as reliable in terms of holding power with their content varying tremendously so that upon scrutiny of the sixteenth and seventeenth century furniture, one finds only hand-cut wooden pegs holding the boards together.

Pegs were chiseled from stringy, sinewy elastic hard woods such as oak, ash and beech. They were never perfectly round and occasionally they were tapered. Although driven tightly into round holes, in time they work their way out, partially due to the shrinkage of the surrounding wood and partially due to the relatively slight shrinkage of the peg itself. (Notice the extended pegs in the old joint stool illustration 190, page 153.) Sometimes a hump (bow) was carved right into the peg. Consequently, when the humped peg was inserted and forced to straighten, the extra pressure from the forced hump would help the peg cling to the mortise and tenon. The humped peg was, in fact, acting like a spring joint.

Some case pieces are made with pegs alone. Pilgrim chairs, tables, and chests were primarily constructed with pegs, as were the Pilgrim houses. The Windsor chair, too, is constructed with pegs and without the aid of glue.

ADHESIVES

Cabinetmakers have also made use of "glue" in the construction of furniture. More properly defined as an adhesive, a substance used for joining or bonding other materials together by surface attachment, glue has been used since prehistoric times. As of the seventeenth century, with the veneering of furniture and use of applied moldings, bosses, and split spindles for decoration, effective glue was essential. It can be safely stated that by the latter part of the seventeenth century, most joints were glued. These first adhesives were probably natural gums and waxes such as resin, rubber, shellac and beeswax, all of which are exuded by certain insects and trees and still find limited use. Very early, the ancient Egyptians employed animal glues in making wood furniture and attaching ornamental veneers to wood surfaces.

The three principal adhesive types are animal and fish ("hide glue"), vegetable, (modern rubber latex and extrine), and the synthetics, so called "white glues." Animal and fish glues are made from hides and bones and are, in fact, an impure form of gelatin. Traditionally (and out of necessity until twenty-five years ago, when a cold liquid hide glue was perfected) animal glue is applied hot and hardens both by cooling and by the absorption or evaporation of water. When evidence of glue is found on furniture up through the nineteenth century, it will necessarily be a form of hide glue, as this was the only kind available.

If furniture appears to have been glued with white glue, this is evidence that the piece has been recently reglued, that it is not very old, or that it may be false requiring further scrutiny. This is because synthetic adhesives were not developed until the 1930's. White glue is by far the strongest of the adhesives used by modern cabinetmakers, is relatively fast-working, and does not deteriorate. Indeed, white glue is so effective that once used on old furniture for repairs, should the damage reoccur, it will be almost impossible to undo early white glue work to make new repairs. It is thus most important that soluable hide glue be used for all glue work on old furniture.

SHOE PIECES

Techniques of joining are the very essence of old furniture construction, and its study is never-ending. Once one has a comfortable understanding of the basic joints, for example, one can identify and muse on the varieties of shoe piece found at the base of the splat, in fact supporting the splat on mid-18th century side chairs. This important member served its function as a separate piece into which the splat was usually mortised at the top, after which the shoe piece was attached to the chair frame. With some chairs the shoe is really two separate pieces, supporting the splat on each side. Occasionally one finds the shoe supporting the splat at its base from behind. Whichever version is used, the shoe will always be there as a separate and necessary part of 18th century period side chairs. Later 18th century style side chairs usually incorporate the shoe function into the back rail as one piece of wood, primarily for reasons of expediency.

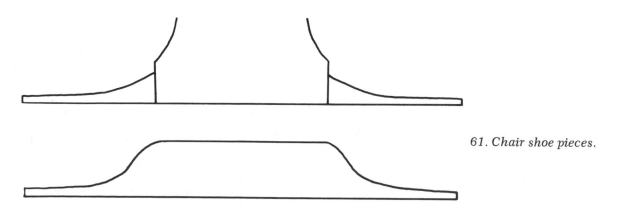

61. *Chair shoe pieces.*

62. *Chair back shoe piece as found on most mid-18th century side chairs. In this example the splat is mortised into this one-piece shoe member which in turn is attached (often nailed) to the top of the back seat rail.*

DRAWER JOININGS

An appropriate conclusion to a discussion about joinings would be a comparison of joined drawers which, by their joining, aid in the dating of a case piece. Starting with the early 17th century drawer, illustrations 63 and 64 show that this drawer is simply lap-jointed at the corners and then nailed to reinforce the joint. (This drawer is also de-

scribed as a "hung" drawer because it moves along on a runner extending from the case interior which fits into the groove cut into the drawer side; hence, the drawer "hangs.") The boards of the bottom, running front to back, were nailed into a rebate in the lower side of the front.

In the late 17th century, the practice of strengthening drawer joints with nails was replaced by the stronger dovetail joint. The introduction of walnut veneered furniture

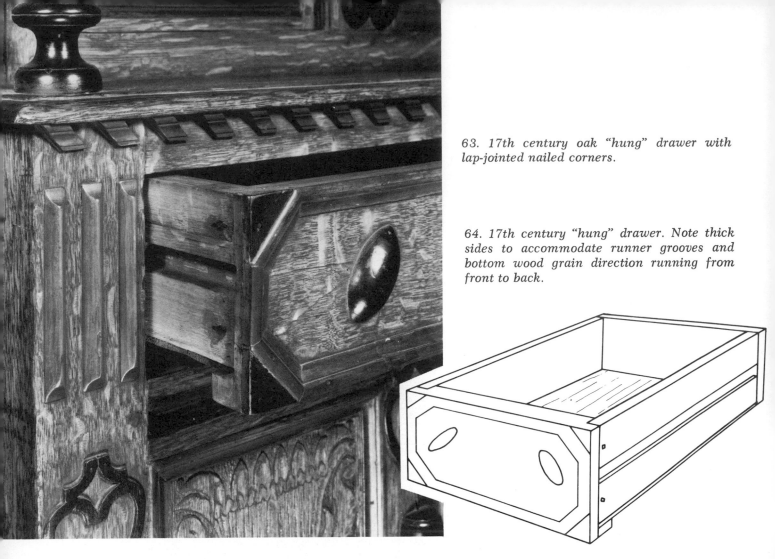

63. 17th century oak "hung" drawer with lap-jointed nailed corners.

64. 17th century "hung" drawer. Note thick sides to accommodate runner grooves and bottom wood grain direction running from front to back.

came at this time and the drawer linings became thinner. This lighter construction was made possible by dispensing with the runner grooves in the drawer sides; this newer drawer slid in and out of the interior on the board forming the drawer bottom. The bottom of the drawer still had the wood grain running from front to back.

With the change to mahogany at about 1720, further drawer construction changes evolved. The single-lapped dovetail joinings became narrower and more numerous. Improvement in the bottom wearing surface consisted of fitting additional pieces of wood to the bottom inside edges of the drawer sides to withstand the friction of wear caused by use. The grain of the bottom then ran side to side, and properly fitted it was glued into the groove in the front and free to swell and shrink at the back. This drawer, often with a lipped front of solid mahogany i.e., the drawer front projecting beyond the core to

which it was fitted (see illustration 194, page 155), was made until about 1750, when veneered fronts of mahogany became more common and cock-bead moldings were applied (rabbeted joining) to the edges of the drawer fronts. This type of drawer is shown on an English secretary (illustration 146, page 117) and on a chest of drawers (illustration 8, page 19).

A further central joining is sometimes used in the drawer bottom when the drawer is particularly wide. By inserting a muntin through the center of the drawer bottom, the joining illustrated, smaller, thinner boards can be used and maximum strength is obtained. At the end of the 18th century and into the 19th century, quarter-round moldings were glued into the interior drawer edges. Again, this served as a form of strength for the joints, but also it eliminated the possibility of dust and grit collecting in the corners.

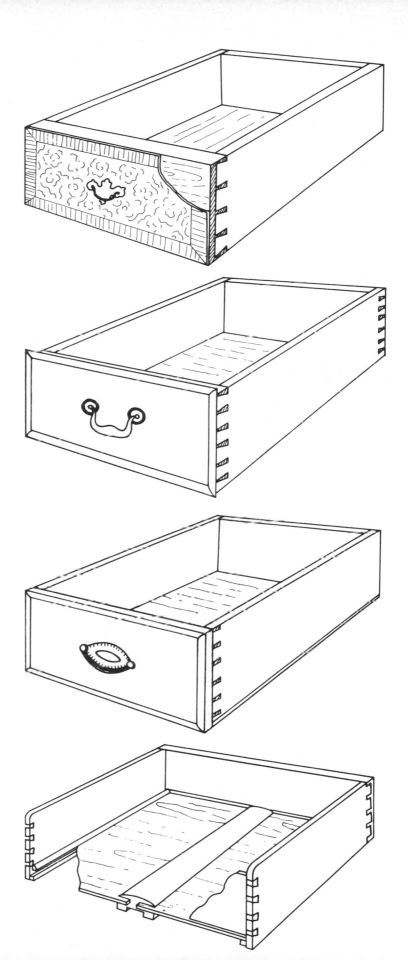

65. *Late 17th century walnut veneer drawer with thinner drawer linings and dovetail joining.*

66. *Lipped solid front mahogany drawer circa 1740. Note fine lapped dovetail joinings and side to side grain direction. The bottom is contained in a groove in front and in rebates in the sides, with strips beneath to widen the bearing surfaces and to prevent the bottom from scraping. The back stands above the bottom.*

67. *Mid-18th century mahogany veneer drawer with cock-bead molding. This molding began in the early 18th century with walnut furniture, and continued in use through the 18th century, though cut with the grain running lengthwise, not crosswise as earlier. The moldings fit at the sides into rebates in the drawer front, the lap of the dovetails being made wide enough to give a reasonable seating for them.*

68. *Late 18th century or early 19th century drawer with muntin partition.*

4

PANELLING AND MOLDINGS

PANELLING

The rectangular panel-within-a-frame form for chest construction appeared in the late 15th century and was generally used for both furniture and architecture in the 16th century. This was joinery in the truest sense: frame and panel construction put together with mortise and tenon joints by the woodworker, now called a joiner. Such construction (see illustration 69) insured that the object would be relatively limited in material, i.e., prior to use of this method, the chest had been composed totally of solid, thick and thus heavy boards. Panel and frame construction required the strength of solid rails and stiles (the horizontal and vertical framing members) with average measurements 2½ to 3 inches wide and 1 to 1½ inches thick. The inner edge grooves of the rails and stiles held the much thinner (and thus lighter) central panels, ⅜ to ¾ inch thickness in the middle, tapering to a $\frac{3}{16}$ inch tongue at the edges. Lightness represented an economy of material but, more importantly, made for easier handling of the final product without loss of strength or utility. In fact, this method allowed for greater flexibility and variety in the use of wood. Suddenly the walls of rooms could be panelled in wood, sometimes 20 feet high, and thus made warmer in winter. The enormous, magnificent Elizabethan beds of the 16th century could never have been created without the relative lightness and resiliency of this form of construction.

The rectangular framing of thin panels had the unique advantage of minimizing the natural acts of warping, splitting, twisting and shrinking, because the panel rested loosely in its grooves in the upright stiles and horizontal rails. Hence it was free to move, to expand and contract with humidity and temperature changes, and to "give" if need be. This elasticity was a deterrent to various forms of bursting. When a panel was not left free to move but was held at the edge(s) and thus could not react to atmospheric conditions, shrinkage cracks and other damage appeared. Notice the left panel in the late 17th century chest (illustration 71). The panel has been held fixed—perhaps the wood swelled tightly into the groove or perhaps dirt and wax filled the groove space so as to secure the panel firmly. Whatever the reason, when shrinkage movement took place, the panel could not move and a crack was the result. Consider as well the example of the secretary door panel (illustration 150, page 120). Shrinkage has moved the panel partially out of its grooved frame. No harm has come to the panel with this method of construction, but, unfortunately, the cabinetmaker has underestimated the possible panel

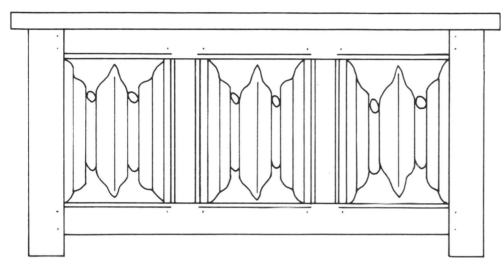

69. Panel and frame construction as here represented with linen-fold pattern carved panels set into the pegged mortise and tenon joined frame of an oak 16th century chest. Note in the vertical section detail how the panel rests freely in its frame thereby having much freedom to expand and contract with atmospheric conditions.

70. An Elizabethan bed of the late 16th century with panelled headboard and tester.

71. 17th century American oak and pine chest of frame and panel construction with shrinkage crack in front panel.

movement in planning the width of his ser-
pentine-shaped upright side stile. Another
example of this flexible construction is the
raised field panel in the painted Swedish cupboard door (illustration 128, page 96), which
has moved without mishap for over 200 years.

Panel and frame construction using mortise and tenon joinery declined in use with
the introduction of veneer work about 1660.
(Where veneer was not intended—for example on tables, chairs, and stools—panel
and frame construction was used.) When a
flat surface was necessary, however, to receive veneer, the uneven panel and frame
surface was not appropriate. Smooth, flat core
stock surfaces for adhering walnut and mahogany veneers were constructed by building up the cores from oak or pine boards
glued side by side; these were trimmed to
shape and secured along the abutting edges
of sides, top and bottom with rows of dovetails set in glue. The exploded chest of
drawers shown in illustration 43, page 40,
describes this jointing procedure beneath the

veneer. Due to broken and missing veneer of
the lower section of a secretary-bookcase,
(illustration 139, page 151), one can see
where the drawer rail has been dovetail jointed
into the abutting side of the case, thereby
maintaining the flat surface of the core
to receive the flat underside of the veneer.
Panel and frame construction was still used
for parts where possible—cabinet and cupboard doors, for example, were worked in
solid wood. An understanding of this form of
construction, along with the different kinds
of moldings and their methods of construction, is very helpful in dating a piece of
furniture.

MOLDINGS

Moldings, scratched in crudely or
achieved with the use of a molding plane
or scratch stock (both having irons cut to the
desired profile) often decorated the edges of

72. Cross-grain walnut applied
cornice moldings characteristic of the 1695 William and
Mary style. The flat surfaces
and large curved surfaces, such
as this center ovolo molding
section, were veneered; the rest
was built up with cross-grained
walnut usually on a softwood
groundwork.

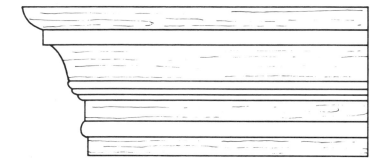

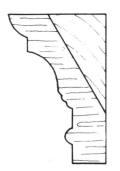

73. *Straight-grain solid molding of mahogany with a backing of softwood.*

the framing (the stiles and rails) around panels. An example of such decoration can be seen in illustration 71. Hence, moldings true to their architectural function of providing decorative treatment enliven plain surfaces with their play of light and shade and accent the lines and design of the furniture.

Moldings in the 17th century were worked in the solid, i.e., the framing edge was being molded. Such a molding moves inward from the surface. Again note illustration 71. During the 17th century it also became customary to decorate furniture with applied moldings (and ornaments such as bosses and split spindles) glued and bradded into position. These moldings projected beyond the surface of the piece, being applied to the structure. The New England 17th century press cupboard drawer shown in illustration 63, page 50, is a dramatic example of this.

Curved moldings at this time were sometimes cut with carving tools, making the surface appreciably irregular; at other times the scratch stock was used, resulting in greater molding surface irregularity. Some applied curved moldings in the late 17th century were large circular arches, and these were turned on a lathe, like a gigantic pair of split spindles. Domed hoods of clock cases and writing cabinet friezes were areas where these large ovolo moldings were frequently applied. Regardless of the tool used and the effect desired, moldings were the result of hand work and hand pressure. Consequently, slight variations can be felt as one passes one's finger along a molding, and these same undulations can be observed if one sights down or along these moldings.

The applied molding reached its height in the 18th century. Such moldings were constructed in a variety of ways. In the Walnut Period, moldings were invariably cross-grained—as with a cross-grained, half-round walnut cornice molding on a William and Mary-style highboy. From the time of mahogany, followed by satinwood, cornice moldings were usually straight-grained and

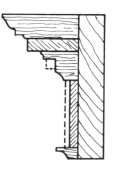

74. *Composite molding built up of several pieces of wood. Note the applied dentil molding and the applied fret. This type of molding is associated with large moldings.*

75. Applied rococo moldings on a 1760–1770 Philadelphia mahogany dressing table of outstanding craftsmanship. Photograph courtesy the Museum of Fine Arts, Boston.

were applied in two forms: 1) with a backing of soft wood, and 2) as a built up composite of several pieces of wood.

Many moldings were carved before being applied. This carving emphasized the characteristic details of the fashion in furniture at the time. Sometimes cornice moldings were carved with the egg and dart detail or acanthus leafage. (Note the gilded, carved molding surrounding the secretary panel in illustration 150, page 120). The rococo moldings applied with glue and nails to Philadelphia Chippendale-style highboys and lowboys are superb and repeat the S and C curves of the cabriole legs and curving pediments.

Another enrichment to the molding

was the applied fret, or superimposed wood tracery, which often serves like an applied carved type of molding, for instance on case pieces as friezes. Then, too, sometimes the fret surface has been carved. Along with the fret, completely cut out before application, is the dentil molding which is executed in a similar way and is usually added under a built up (composite) cornice. (See illustration 74.)

The cock-bead molding, added frequently to accent drawer front edges starting about 1750, was another handsome form of molding. An example of this can be seen in the photographed secretary-bookcase drawers (illustration 146, page 117). This half-round convex molding was an important style characteristic for a short while and thus becomes a helpful dating consideration.

All these types of strikingly executed applied moldings made unique forms of furniture decoration passible, and many of the moldings endeavored to suggest completeness with the piece. There were, in fact, solid moldings during the 18th century, as illustrated in the tea table detail here. The crack clearly shows the molded rim to be a continuous part of the table top. So-called pie-

crust tea tables (see illustration 36, page 32), also have a solid carved rim molding, the center surface of the table having been dished out and planed smooth.

The delicate moldings of the Hepplewhite-Sheraton period were occasionally inlaid with contrasting woods in keeping with the refined use of veneers and inlays in classical and delicate designs of this style. Notice such moldings on the satinwood knife box, illustration 9, page 19.

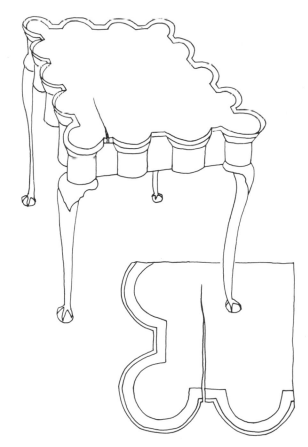

76. *Corner of scallop-edged mahogany tea table, Boston, circa 1750, with cracked tray top.*

77. *Scallop-edge tea table with detailed corner. The table top is anchored to the table frame on all four sides causing shrinkage strain.*

The small, semi-circular raised center astragal molding of solid wood is again the product of the molding plane; occasionally it was hand carved. It was frequently applied to glazing bars of bookcases and cabinet glass doors in the late 18th century. Using glass in doors was a special feature during this period, hence decorative molding both caught the eye and served the function of supporting the glass in place. A refined example of an astragal molding appears in the photograph of the secretary-bookcase, illustration 126, page 93.

Finally, there is the tapered bead molding found on Hepplewhite-style square tapering legs and on the tapered saber legs of Regency-style chairs and tripod table bases. The leg is wider at the top and the molding appears to become increasingly narrow as the leg tapers to the floor. To achieve this graduation of spacing, the scratch stock was used with the same cutter on each side to confine the tapering to the center raised area. That is to say, the beaded edges are the same width all along the edges and all gradation takes place in the center of the member.

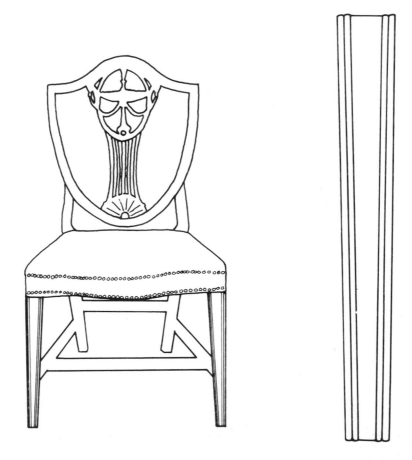

78. Hepplewhite-style chair and chair leg showing apparently tapered molding.

5

CURVED FORMS

THE DEFINITION OF A CURVE is a continuously bending line without angles. This rounded flowing line in a piece of furniture attracts and leads the eye, and it is little wonder that the use of curving forms is frequently adopted by cabinetmakers. Consider, for example, the beauty of the long, delicately restrained, curving necks of the swan head terminals on both sides of the American Empire-style parlor easel shown here.

Almost any furniture part can be curved in form: chair legs, arms, scrolled feet, ogee bracket feet, sweeping broken Roman pediment bonnet tops to highboys and certain moldings—ogee, ovolo etc. It should also be noted that the curve possesses infinite variety and degree. Well known to furniture scholars is Hogarth's "line of beauty" analysis in which the celebrated painter and engraver, William Hogarth (1697–1764), evaluated a series of proportions for the cyma curve, a continuous double curve, one part being convex and the other part concave. He concluded in this 1753 *Analysis of Beauty* that only one precise configuration of "waving line" should be deemed *the* line of beauty. He visually supports his conclusion with a comparison of waving lines, the Line of Beauty and Grace being No. 4, and he applies the Line to all subjects including chair legs, corsets and turned candlestick stems.

The cabinetmaker had several alternative ways to produce a curved form, depending on the function of the furniture part involved. The swan neck terminals shown above have

been carved into their curving form and then applied to the easel frame. (Note as well the delicately carved feathers.) The scrolled, curving Flemish foot found on a Carolean-style chair or stool also represents careful planning and execution by the carver. (Such a foot can be seen on the stool in illustration 192, page 154.) The continuous cyma and reverse cyma curves that make up the so-called "French edge" or "crows beak and scroll" edge found on mid-18th century round tea tables are further examples of handsome carved ornamentation. Notice the silhouette of this forceful curving edge on the table top (illustration 177, page 140).

The curving form is often incorporated in the structural parts of a piece of furniture. To be successful, this required tremendous skill and planning on the part of the cabinet-maker. Many examples of such successful accomplishments remain as our heritage to-day; again one marvels at the capabilities of cabinetmakers of the past. The cabriole leg, so-called from the French word *capriole*, meaning a caper or leap (derived from a dressage movement during which a horse leaves the ground with his forelegs tucked under and his hind legs extended in a horizontal position), is a leg curving in two directions and involving both cyma and reverse cyma curves (see illustration 130, page 99). The challenge of the proportions of this leg is enormous, and the planning of the wood requirement, the over-all curving design, and the execution carving were all products of the master cabinetmaker's skill. The restrained classical sweeping curve of a saber leg, Regency-style chair, as fashionable in the early 19th century, suggests these same master craftsman concerns and abilities.

The bombé (or outline form swelling towards the base, sometimes described as kettle shape) case pieces made in 17th century Holland and 18th century New England (especially the Boston area) employed the curving form as their major motif and outline. Such pieces demanded complicated planning and execution on the part of the cabinetmaker. In fact, they were so difficult to accomplish that there are few known successful examples. Keep in mind, as you consider

79. *Swan head terminals showing use of curved forms. Photograph courtesy the Museum of Fine Arts, Boston.*

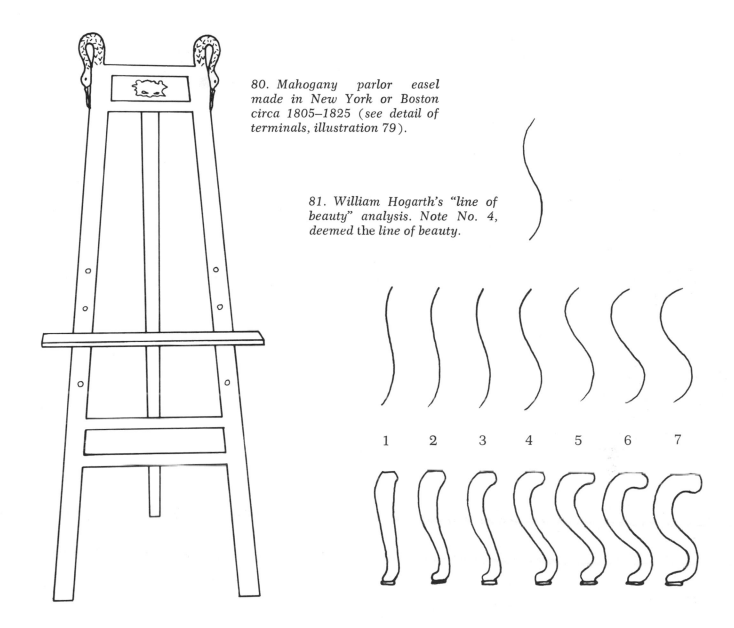

80. Mahogany parlor easel made in New York or Boston circa 1805–1825 (see detail of terminals, illustration 79).

81. William Hogarth's "line of beauty" analysis. Note No. 4, deemed the line of beauty.

1   2   3   4   5   6   7

the illustrations of a bombé chest of drawers shown here, that to achieve the swelling curved sides requires a thickness of wood adequate to include the fullness of the curve, which then must be carved out to create this movement. In turn the drawer fronts involve similar work, as they swell outward in a different but related direction.

The ogee bracket foot (illustration 88, page 67), is a bracket foot whose outline suggests the ogee classical molding—a double curve, convex above and concave below. Again, the cabinetmaker has carved this curving structural form from solid wood, and he has succeeded in adopting the graceful flowing beauty of the curving line for the

82. *Four-drawer chest of drawers of bombé form, probably by John Cogswell of Boston, circa 1770–1790. The drawers made of crotch figure mahogany veneered on straight-grained mahogany have an applied bead molding. Photograph courtesy the Museum of Fine Arts, Boston.*

83. *Bombé swelling outline form, both at the side and on the front. Note how the side lines of the drawers also conform to the swell of the case.*

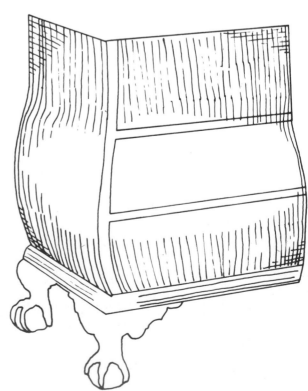

functional furniture part, thus creating a graceful but sturdy foot—one of the most handsome in furniture history.

No consideration of curved structural forms would be complete without considering the many curves found in chair backs and the dramatic and graceful effects they create. The serpentine curved chair rail of a Chippendale-style chair, the delicately sweeping curves of a shield-shaped back of a late 18th century style chair, and the smooth rounded back of the semi-gondola bergère chair of the early French Empire style all recall the carver's skills. Many times these included the art of compound curvature, i.e., the carving out of shapes which curve in both front and side elevation, or in elevation and plan. Again the cabriole leg comes to mind, as do the early 18th century chair backs, some of which were shaped in front elevation, side elevation and also plan (Queen Anne-style chairs, for instance). The cabinetmaker and/or carver needed to make these curves satisfactory from several directions.

To carve curved forms from solid wood is certainly an extravagant use of fine wood in that the curves require large thick boards to meet the required thickness for the curve. This in turn produces much wasted wood when it is cut away to produce the curve. The technique of veneer generated an alternative method for producing such pieces as bow-front and serpentine-front chests of drawers and commodes and, by the late 18th century, this method was frequently used. The technique was one of building up the desired curvature of the core stock with a series of small pieces of wood—sometimes called bricks—and then applying veneer to the exterior surface. Illustration 85 of a bow-fronted chest of drawers demonstrates this method. The entire curving front is made up of small pieces of wood glued together in brick-laying fashion, with the vertical joints over-lapping for maximum strength. In addition to little wood being used and wasted, the grain direction of the individual bricks follows the curve, thereby exposing a minimum of end grain on the surface. (Exposed end grain does not absorb glue or stain well

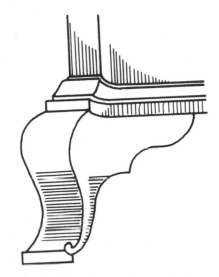

84. *Ogee bracket foot. The curled scroll on the inside of this foot is a characteristic 18th century Newport Goddard-Townsend cabinet-making motif, unique to their block front ogee feet.*

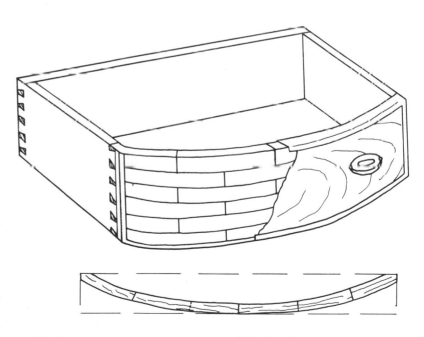

85. *Drawer core curvature created in brick-laying fashion.*

or evenly which leads to veneer adhering problems.)

A variation of this technique, sometimes called coopering, is a vertical application— for curving doors of hanging corner cupboards and for the curving doors of Louis XV-style French commodes, for example. Long narrow strips are jointed together on a working cradle into the desired curving shape. Clamping boards at the top and bottom of the door hold the long boards in place, thereby minimizing future movement and warping. These developed surfaces are finally covered with decorative veneer.

Examples suggesting these techniques are the bow-front mahogany veneered chest of drawers (illustration 8, page 19) and the satinwood veneered knife box (illustration 9, page 19) with its curving front projection. Application of the coopering technique, working horizontally, can be recognized in

86. Bow-back Windsor chair with back and arm all one curving piece.

the curving delicate veneered cylinder fall found on French Directoire-style cylinder writing tables or bureaux of the late 18th century.

Sometimes the "brick building" technique is passed over for the straightforward approach of carving the curved parts in the solid, and carefully applying them to the finished surface of the piece with no intention of veneer. A superb example of this would be handsomely carved and proportioned convex blocks and scallop shells applied to the case pieces made by the Goddard-Townsend cabinetmakers. The Edmund Townsend kneehole desk (illustration 202, page 164) has applied shells and blocks, as does the John Goddard style secretary-bookcase (illustration 120, page 89). Turned split spindles applied to 17th century cupboards with glue and nails are also examples of solid curving form decoration applied to the surface of the piece.

After these difficult and sophisticated techniques for incorporating curved forms into and onto furniture, let us appreciate two very straightforward and effective methods. The first is simply cutting out the outline of the desired curve from flat wood or boards with a fretsaw. The resulting flat wood silhouette is then applied or included as part of the piece of furniture. The Chippendale-style looking glass with its elaborate scrolling apron and cresting is a good example of cut out flat wood. (Note the outline of the looking glass, illustration 214, page 175.) Thicker wood serving a structural purpose, but cut in the same way, is exemplified in the curving scrolling foot of the late 19th century table (illustration 125, page 92).

The curving shape of the broken Roman pediment style "bonnet top" highboy is again the product of cutting flat wood by saw. The outline shape of the scrolling pediment as seen from the front derives from one large piece of cut wood. The curved solid shape which follows the shape of the "front" pediment elevation and extends the depth of the piece (called the "bonnet" or "hooded

*87. The 1859 Thonet Nr 14 chair consisting
of six parts—a long beechwood rod bent into
a loop to form the back legs and chair back,
a smaller loop to fit inside this and give extra
support to the back, a hoop to form the framework for a caned seat, a smaller hoop to go
below as a stretcher, and two tapering bent
rods for the front legs. It was cheap to make,
light, and transportable in parts to be assembled anywhere with less than ten screws
—joints have been entirely eliminated.*

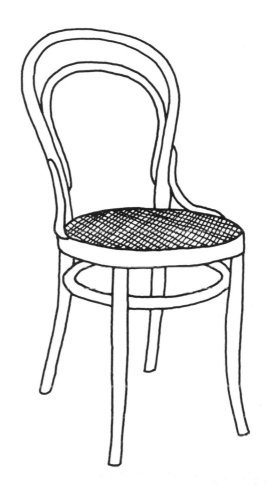

pediment") is the result of small flat pieces
of wood being cut and jointed together and
glued at right angles to the broken pediment
front, following the curve of its outline. This
delicate structure is sometimes supported by
a cover of canvas glued over it. (See the
broken pediment examples in illustration 31,
page 30 and illustration 201, page 163.)

A second simple and direct method for
producing curved forms is the technique of
bending wood. The bent or curved permanent
shape is caused by subjecting the wood to
heat or moisture under pressure. The bowed
back of a Windsor chair represents one of
the earliest forms of such bending. Hickory,
oak, ash (or yew in England) with their pliable quality were used for this purpose, often
in green state. The members (hoop backs
and spur stretchers) were first planed to the
necessary size and section and then steamed
or soaked in water until bendable. Each was
then clamped in a form made of wood or
metal of required shape and allowed to dry.
When dry, the member retained its curvature.
Some of the delicate galleried 18th century
tea tables of serpentine shape have the gallery rail bent into the conforming serpentine
shape of the table top (see illustration 91,
page 71).

Michael Thonet (1796–1871) perfected
and developed the bentwood technique into
an entire style of furniture. Beechwood was
used for the Thonet process because it was
resilient and had long fibers and few knots.
The trunks were mechanically sawn into
strips about 1″ square and then turned on a
lathe, becoming circular in section. Place-
ment in autoclaves for steaming rendered
them pliable and then they were bent around
metal forms and so kept until completely dry.
Final shaping and finishing made the individual curved or bent parts ready for "mass
production" assembly and sales distribution.
Awareness of the machine with its vast capabilities and speed brought many new ideas
and techniques to the furniture maker. Har-
nessing machinery for such uses as creating
curving forms led to highly original and ex-
perimental furniture by the mid-19th century.

6

CARVING AND FRETWORK

CARVING

The carving of wood by hand—using special tools (chisels, gouges, files, saws and smoothing instruments) to cut three-dimensional forms out of solid wood—dates back to antiquity and has served utilitarian and decorative purposes ever since. The rich life-size carved fruit and flowers on large chests and cupboards of Renaissance Italy come immediately to mind as exuberant examples of the carver's abilities. The variety in subject, detail and scale is endless, as is the pleasure in exploring any one example for the foibles of hand craftsmanship and the ingenuity and control of the skilled carver. Feast your eyes on the superb carving on the chamfered ogee bracket foot by Samuel McIntire of Salem, Massachusetts, executed on a late 18th century chest on chest. The low relief acanthus leaves are delicately but carefully rendered with a variety of carving techniques, such as incising, under-cutting, veining, fluting and smoothing. These are set off by the star-punched background, a kind of carving McIntire favored, judging from the frequency with which it is found on the known examples of his work.

The mid-18th century was a peak era for carving as the major form of furniture decoration. The carving of the Renaissance had

set the standard and served as inspiration from then on. The 18th century drew extensively from this in its adaptations and rococo interpretations. Again in the mid-19th century, high relief elaborate carving was revived for furniture ornamentation.

A great impetus for extensive carving during the 1740's, 1750's and 1760's was the discovery and adoption of mahogany. This beautiful rich wood was not only extremely strong, thereby allowing the Chippendale style to evolve with its delicate legs and precarious parts, but it could be successfully carved. (Walnut, in comparison, tended to splinter and hence was rarely carved.) 18th century carvers revelled in scrolled acanthus leafwork, nullings, masks, cabochons, shells and interlacing scrolls and straps. Later, less robust Sheraton-style carving included classical subjects, vases, festoons, drapery swags and wheat husks, along with reeding and fluting.

LOW VERSUS HIGH RELIEF

By their innate nature, carved details are an integral part of the solid wood from which they have been carved. When the cabinet-maker-carver was concerned with low-relief carving, an example of which is found on the 17th century panelled chest (illustration 71, page 53), his wood thickness requirement was little altered since the shallow carving and incised lines did not penetrate deeply. He could even change his patterns and carving plans after the chest was joined because the carving was flat and flush with the surface of the piece and its depth was shallow and uniform regardless of chosen pattern.

Carving in greater relief, however, demanded extensive pre-planning in the choice of wood for the specific carved detail and for the part of furniture for which it was intended. The Tudor linenfold panel, for example, carved to represent a piece of folded linen, required thickness in the center and thinness at the edges to enable the panel to fit into the grooves of the framing. (See the panel thickness drawing, illustration 69, page 53.)

The cabriole leg with knee carving was a great challenge for any furniture carver, past or present. To start with, it is awkward to work out the shape on paper—i.e., since the leg is seen from several sides, including from above, it is impossible to draw on paper all the angles for which to plan. Therefore, templetes or patterns of thin wood were used to mark out the curves on adjacent faces on the square block of wood. (A templete enabled many legs to be marked out alike and thus matched.) As the carving progressed and the rounded leg began to emerge from the original rectangular shape, the guiding lines on the wood were cut away using frame saw and spokeshave. Everything is curved in both directions. The project became even more complicated when carving was to appear on the knee, because additional thickness of stock

88. Chamfered ogee bracket foot. Photograph courtesy the Museum of Fine Arts, Boston.

had to be planned. The presence of these plain blocks could distract the carver, giving a false impression of the shape as a whole. It is thus little wonder that beautifully shaped cabriole legs are rare to find and see.

The recognition of wood requirements for additional decorative carving alerts one against shallow carving of later date—often undertaken to add to the interest and value of the piece. This is called "carving up." Often, plain cabriole legs have carved details added to the knees. This carving will always seem surprisingly shallow in proportion to the leg, because no extra wood has been left at the knee to allow for the carving to project attractively from the main curve of the leg. An example of this can be seen in illustration 195, page 156.

SHELL CARVING

Carving takes many forms. Different techniques produce a variety of effects. Much depends on the goal—which becomes a cabinetmaking decision and choice. Carved convex and concave shells were often the focus of design and attention on block front case furniture by the Goddard-Townsend families during the 1760's. (See the Edmund Townsend knee-hole desk, illustration 202, page 164 and the detailed convex shell on the fall front of the secretary-bookcase, illustration 120, page 89, attributed to John Goddard.) Many of these shells along with the blocking were carved from one solid piece of wood. Other blocks and shells were carved and then applied. (Both the desk and the secretary-bookcase mentioned above have applied shells and blocks.) One way to determine the presence of applied work is to follow the wood grain—if it is continuous, only one piece of wood is involved. Another way is to look for join lines.

REEDING AND FLUTING

Reeding (or carved ribbing made up of half-round "reeds" grouped side by side) and fluting (parallel vertical grooves separated slightly by an edge in between which derives from the classical column) are types of carving that by their use of repetition brought emphasis and detail to chair legs, bed posts and pilasters on the sides of case pieces. Fluting was always cut out of the surface of the wood, using gouges. Reeding was usually cut into the wood with a scratch stock.

FINIALS AND PENDANTS

Carved finials (eagles, flames, urns, etc.) found on highboys, chest on chests and tall clocks stand as three-dimensional sculptures in their own right. Consider the elegant cartouche so often identified with the Connecticut cabinetmaker Eliphalet Chapin, working between 1771–1795. Pendants, the smaller carved ornaments that point downward and are usually found attached to the aprons of lowboys and highboys, represent further examples of this form of carving.

Finials and pendants were carved separately and then attached with glue. Since glue unfortunately can lose its power with time, this type of attached ornamental work has, in many cases, fallen out and been lost. Often finials have not even been glued into position but fitted loosely into their tenons for easy, safe removal should the piece be moved. It is thus not surprising to discover foreign finials on old pieces (where someone has exercised "make do" with what they had), no finials at all, or sometimes new replacement finials. Finials and pendants should always be carefully examined to determine their relationship to the rest of the piece.

CARVING WITH GESSO

This is one kind of carving in which the details are only roughly chiseled out in the wood. No attempt at finishing refinement is made, because the entire piece is coated with layers of whiting, called gesso, to a thickness of about ¼ inch. When the whiting dries, the carver wets the gesso with a brush and finishes his designs by carving highlights into the gesso surface. The entire piece is then gilded or painted. Note the damaged hand rest of a French gilded chair (illustration 134, page 102) showing the layers of wood, gesso, and gold leaf. This treatment has also been used for the frames of many 18th century looking glasses. One often suspects gesso-work to have been the original treatment when one comes across a piece of furniture of fine pro-

89. Decorative cartouche finial.

portions and cabinetwork but remarkably poor carving. *Has* the piece been stripped of its original gesso-carved refinement?

PIERCED CARVING

Sometimes carving not only decorates the surface of the wood but the carving (or cutting) is taken right through the wood for even greater decorative effect. This is called piercing or pierced carving and many examples of this technique can be cited. See, for example, the Carolean chair back (illustration 148, page 118) which incorporates piercing to emphasize the circular lines of the leafage and scrolls. Some pediments atop highboys produce a light, lattice-like effect because of piercing, as in illustration 89. The carved and pierced chair back splats of Chippendale-and Hepplewhite-style chairs with their dramatic silhouettes represent the extent

to which this technique has been taken. In fact, the strength and function of the chair becomes effected (even threatened) as a result of such elaborate working of one wooden splat back. (Note the damaged chair splat back in illustration 174, page 138.)

CARVER'S PIECES

True "carver's pieces" as opposed to the categories of case pieces and seat furniture, were pieces that did not have a useful function, like chairs, and hence lent themselves for the display of the carver's fantasies and abilities. These highly decorative objects would include girandoles, looking glass frames, side and console tables and candlestands. Examples of all kinds and combinations of carving can be found on these pieces and, indeed, the carver's talents are wonderfully demonstrated.

90. *A carver's piece. One of a pair of carved and gilded girandoles in the 18th century English rococo style. It closely follows the design of Plate No. CLXXVIII in Thomas Chippendale's* Gentleman & Cabinetmakers' Director *(3rd ed.) 1762. Photograph courtesy the Museum of Fine Arts, Boston.*

FRETWORK

Fretwork should not be confused with pierced carving. Fretwork, i.e., perforated decoration, is indeed a form of open work and sometimes is used in solid three-dimensional form—such as a fretwork stretcher on a Chinese Chippendale-style chair. However, fretwork, sometimes called cut work, involves a technique of its own.

Fretwork is usually composed of small geometrical interlacings, resembling trellis-work. In solid form, it serves as a structural detail—galleries to table tops and open work stretchers for chairs and tables. As applied decoration to a solid ground (sometimes referred to as blind frets)—friezes of tables and highboys and for chair legs during the vogues of the Chinese and Gothic Chippendale styles —fretwork served strictly as a form of applied ornamentation. Other forms of applied carved ornamentation are rosettes terminating the scrolls of a broken Roman pedimented

highboy, "curved streamers" on Philadelphia mid-18th century mahogany furniture, and many kinds of applied moldings. An example of applied fretwork for a frieze can be noted in illustration 74 on page 55. The tea table shown in illustration 91 displays a fretwork gallery.

Fretwork is occasionally cut out of the solid wood and as such is a straightforward form of incised geometric carving. Some fretwork is cut from a single board; the design is cut out with a fret saw and then is glued onto its planned location. Most fretwork, however, is of laminated construction—three thicknesses of mahogany glued together. This lamination of three or more layers, with the grain of the center layer at right angles to the other two, created greater strength for the fragile fret. (See the close-up detail of the top of a fret gallery in illustration 91.) Lamination in this early form also lent its inherent stability, i.e., minimum movement, to these delicate constructions. Even so, it is rare to find structural fretwork totally intact without repairs and replacements.

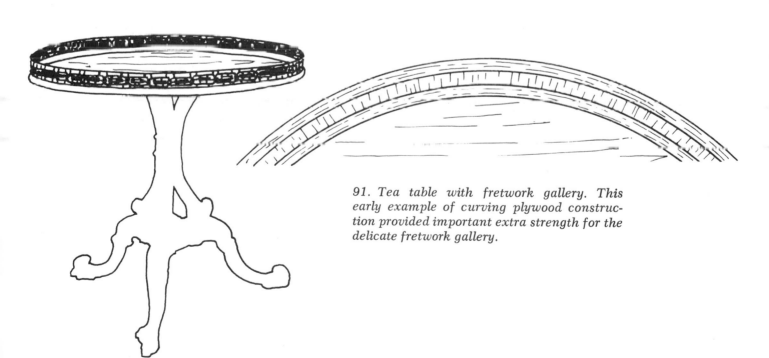

91. Tea table with fretwork gallery. This early example of curving plywood construction provided important extra strength for the delicate fretwork gallery.

CHAPTER
7

NAILS AND SCREWS

NAILS

HAND-WROUGHT NAILS

From the Roman hand-forged "clavus" (found in excavations and sunken ships dating to 500 A.D.), through the 17th and 18th century "sparrabels," "clinkers" and "roses," and into the 19th century, nails were made by hand, one by one, by skilled "nailers." Furniture makers have always made occasional use of nails in their work. The first hand-wrought nails in the United States were imported from England, although, by the late 17th century, rolling and slitting mills which produced nail rods (rectangular strips or rods of malleable iron several feet long and about a quarter of an inch thick) had been built from Maine to Virginia.

The nail rods were cut and forged by hand into nails. The nailmaker, who may have been a professional or perhaps a farmer who needed nails to build a barn, heated one end of the nail rod in his forge and then, on the anvil, pointed it with the hammer on all four sides to the thickness and taper required. He then partly cut through the rod, above the point, inserted the pointed end in a hole of the proper size in a swage block, broke off the rod along the partial cutting, and hammered down the projecting end so as to spread it around the top of the hole to form a head.

After the new nail cooled and shrank, it was easily knocked out of the swage block. The physical characteristics of the handmade nail, therefore, are the roundish crested heads formed by hammer blows and the long irregularly tapered squared shanks usually ending in points.

Many varieties and sizes of nails were wrought in this manner, ranging from huge spikes for shipbuilding to small nails for securing moldings and brasses on furniture. The furniture nail, less than 1″ in length and with a small flat head, or no head, is sometimes referred to as a "finish nail," and is relatively fine, as can be seen in the comparison photo. The names of other nail shapes include deck, clasp, cloat, cooper, clench, dog and horseshoe. Little evidence is available, however, for providing accurate dating for any of these variations.

Handmade nails were strong and tough and had long lives. The purity of the iron and the density of the texture (produced by hand-forging) made them highly resistant to rust and dampness. Because of the time, effort and skill required to produce each nail, nails were a very precious commodity and the same nails were used again and again.

Hand-wrought nails are most often found in case pieces, particularly where early furniture makers used them to hold backboards in place. Early American Bible boxes, six-board

92. *Early nails. Top to bottom,
furniture finishing nail with
side-hammered L-shaped head;
hand-wrought nail with convex-
hammered-round head; cut-nail
before hammered head application; cut-nail with square machine-stamped head, one operation.*

93. *Rough back of chest of drawers secured to core stock with old nails. Note later but old canvas strip covering and holding the shrunken boards together.*

chests, blanket chests and early drawers were usually nailed (see the 17th century press cupboard drawer, illustration 63, page 50 and the nailed backside of the desk box, illustration 23, page 26), as were large architectural pieces such as corner cupboards. Nails were also used in the upholstering of chairs (see illustration 94) and as a means of decorating upholstery. This can be seen in the Copley portrait in which the artist confirms the use of large brass nailheads to enhance the chair. When old nails do appear, they are helpful evidence in approximating the age of the piece because all nails were entirely hand-forged until almost 1800. For example, the likely date of the iron plate at the base of the tripod table pedestal (shown in illustration 123, page 91), is reinforced by the likely date of supporting nails.

CUT-NAILS

The more easily produced machine-cut nail, called a cut-nail, had superseded the use of wrought nails everywhere by the early 1800's because it was so much cheaper. Two cut-nail factories had been established in Philadelphia by 1797. The cut-nail consists of a rectangular tapering shank of iron, not

94. A barrel-back Hepplewhite-style chair frame, stripped of its upholstery. In the wing upper corner detail, many rows of nail holes can be seen, made by upholstery nails of the past—a chair of this date, about 1795, would have likely been reupholstered several times in its history.

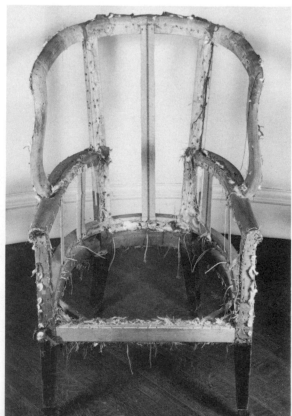

95. Portrait of Mrs. Isaac Smith by John Singleton Copley, painted in 1769. Large brass nailheads were used to ornament such large 18th century richly upholstered arm chairs. Photograph courtesy the Yale University Art Gallery. Gift of Maitland Fuller Griggs.

hammered into a point by hand, but tapered by a single angle cut across a plate of iron. The blacksmith was thus furnished with a strip of plate iron, several feet in length, about 2¼ inches wide and usually about ⅛ inch thick. The strip slid into a cutter, which, rising and falling rapidly, clipped off the end of the iron plate crosswise into narrow tapering rectangular slices—or nails. The taper of the cut produced the point of the nail. The nail head was made by dropping the freshly cut piece, point downward, into a slotted clamp or vise, and then spreading the larger projecting end with a hammer as in the case of the wrought nail. Hammer-headed cut-nails thus required two operations. They date from 1800–1825 and hence are occasionally found used in furniture made during this time.

By 1825, the cut-nail machine had been perfected so as to enable cut-nails to be made by a single operation in one machine, in which the machine cut the nail, clamped it, and, in a single blow of great pressure to the

end of the nail, formed the head by the displacement of metal. The earliest stamped heads (1825–1830) were thin, lopsided and imperfect but became thicker, square and more regular after 1830.

Both hammer-headed cut-nails and machine-headed cut-nails are easily distinguished from hand-wrought nails. Cut and wrought nails both have rectangular shanks, but the wrought nails taper on four sides—the cut-nail only on two opposite sides. The cut-nail will be as thick at the point as at the head—in fact the thickness of the nail plate from which it was cut. Furthermore, the two cut sides of the cut-nail show minute parallel striations or burrs, absent on the wrought nail, which mark the down smear of the cutter. However, it is interesting to note that the newly invented cut-nail was too brittle to clench and could not compete with the strength of its handmade predecessor for such things as gates, doors, wagon bodies and boats; thus hand-forged nail production continued for another century.

In about 1870, the modern, machine-made steel wire nail with its round head and circular shank made its general appearance. It was manufactured earlier in the 19th century in Europe, but American wire nail machinery was not perfected until the 1860's—machinery for this purpose was exhibited at the 1876 Centennial Exhibition in Philadelphia. The earliest wire nails can be distinguished from their modern counterparts by their heads being bulbous and generally eccentric with respect to their shanks. Wire nails do not represent age earlier than the late 19th century, and when found in a seemingly older piece of furniture, indicate late 19th or 20th century repairs, alterations, or maintenance.

SCREWS

HANDMADE SCREWS

Screws were handmade as of about 1700 and were much more scarce than nails during the 18th century. The cutting of the thread without the benefit of steel dies required a great deal of time, patience and skill, making

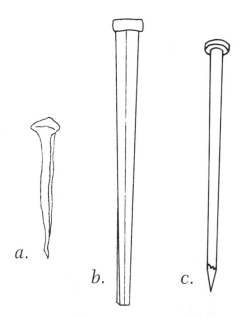

96. *Nail Forms. The hand-wrought nail (a) tapers on four sides; the cut-nail (b) tapers on two opposite sides; the machine-made wire nail (c) has a circular shank and tapers continuously.*

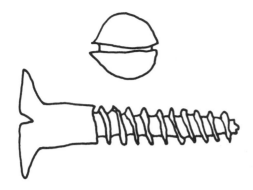 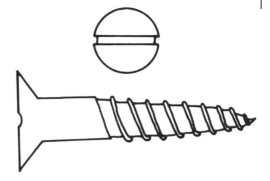

97. Hand-made (left) and modern (right) screws showing head slots.

screws a very expensive item for the provincial cabinetmaker. When the machine-cut screw made its appearance around 1812, it not only proved cheaper, but was more effective, thereby bringing handmade production to a quick end.

Screws, as well as nails, are a guide to dates and thus age. 18th century screws were handmade and can be easily recognized. Studying an early iron or brass screw, one can see that the spiral thread of the shank (sometimes called the worm) was hand-cut with a file. The threads are thus uneven and rounded rather than sharp. There is practically no taper to the shaft and the ends were cut off square. The slots in the heads, made with a hacksaw, were shallow, narrow, irregular and sometimes slightly off center. This handmade screw is compared with a modern screw in illustrations 97 and 98.

Early handmade screws with their extra strength capacity (when compared with nails) had many important uses. Table tops have always been attached to their frames or legs with screws. (Note the old screws in the underside of the table in illustration 177, page 140.) All hinges required and contained screws since screws, unlike nails, did not need clinching (i.e., turning over the point) to hold the hinge and thus did not disfigure the surface on drop-leaf tables and other concealed hinge locations. (See the hinge in illustration 108, page 82.) Locks were secured with screws. The backs of case pieces were sometimes screwed rather than nailed to the core stock. Chest of drawer tops were often screwed down. Obviously all screw-in knobs involved screws—the tiny brass knobs on the

little drawers behind the fall of an 18th century secretary immediately come to mind. Cornerblocks, important in the construction of chairs, were sometimes screwed into place.

MACHINE-CUT SCREWS

The machine-cut metal screw was made for a short time between 1815 and 1845. This was a relatively uniform screw with a blunt end, even screw threads and a round even head. Made in a factory with steam engine power, there were five operations involved—the cutting of the wire to the correct length, the forging of the head, the turning of the head and upper part of the shank, the cutting of the notch and the cutting of the thread.

The modern "gimlet-point" (pointed end)

*98. Left: Hand-made screw.
Right: Modern "gimlet-point" screw.*

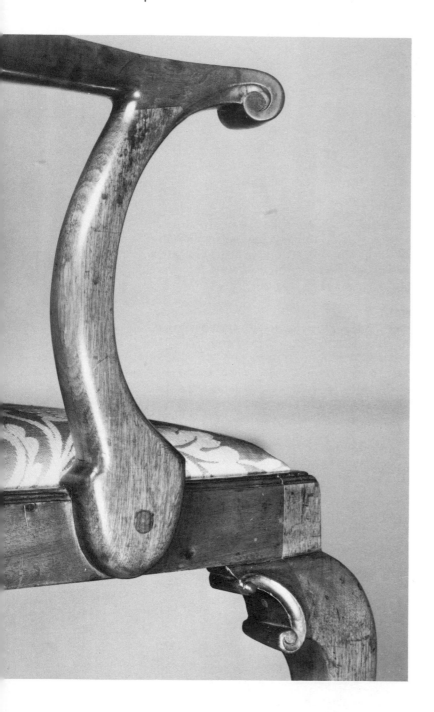

metal screw dates from the Great Exhibition of 1851. Modern metal screws in old furniture therefore suggest either replacement or that the piece was made after 1851. The screws securing a hinge or lock are likely to be replaced; elsewhere, replacement is less probable. The likelihood of a screw which has been in place for a century or more coming loose and falling out, thus requiring replacement by a modern screw, is remote without special movement at that part. Replacement screws are relatively easy to remove, and upon examination of the hole from which the screw has been removed, two sets of screw threads should be apparent, proving the replacement of an earlier screw. Furthermore, screws, like nails, rust with changes in temperature and humidity, hence early screws will have stained the wood around them. Note the 17th century drawer nail and the surrounding wood (illustration 63, page 50).

It should be observed that on a good piece of furniture no two screws (or nails) will be inserted on the same line, a precaution taken to avoid splitting the wood along the lines of its grain. It should also be noted that 18th century cabinetmakers used colored beeswax to conceal screw heads and nailheads. The Victorian cabinetmakers preferred wooden plugs for this purpose, attempting to match the direction of the grain, color and wood of the plug to the surround as much as possible. An example of such a wooden plug can be seen in the photographed Chippendale-style chair where the arm support is screwed to the seat rail.

99. Detail of arm chair showing use of the wooden plug to disguise the screw head. Earlier 18th century cabinetmakers generally used screws from the inside out hence there would have been no need for such concealment.

8

HARDWARE AND ACCESSORIES

FURNITURE HARDWARE AND ACCESSORIES provide an excellent source of supporting information as to the age of a piece of furniture. They should always receive careful examination by the student of antique furniture.

HINGES

Hinges are a basic functional element in the construction of furniture, at the same time often serving as a means of decoration.

PIN HINGE AND STRAP HINGE

Wooden pin hinges date back to the 12th and 13th century chests. Hand-wrought iron hinges were also in general use at this time, particularly for heavily strapped chests (see illustration 7, page 18), some of the straps on the lid being finished off to form part of the hinge. The oldest type of strap hinge did not have a pin; the tongue was simply pulled through a slot in the shorter plate and bent over. (This is sometimes described as the wrapped joint of such a hinge.) However, by the middle of the 18th century, the strong strap hinges were made with pins and continue in this basic form today. Strap hinges, often with chamfered edges—especially in England—are known in many shapes. The "cocks-head" shaped hinge of 17th century

England and the "H" and "L" hinges of 18th century England and Colonial America are examples.

COTTER PIN HINGE

Larger cotter pins of hand-wrought iron, linked together by inserting one through the loop of the other (sometimes called staple hinges) were another early form of hinge often used for the lids of blanket chests and bible boxes. The pairs of pointed ends, made from the interlocking iron loops, went through the top and back of a chest and were turned over or "clinched" into the wood. This was not a terribly durable arrangement, though simple and serviceable, and most of these hinges worked loose or broke. Evidence of their earlier presence remains, nevertheless, and this is a welcome sign of authenticity.

BUTTERFLY HINGE

So-called because the leaves when open flare out from the pin like the wings of a butterfly, the butterfly hinge was widely used up through 1750 and often had edges that were thinner than the main body of the hinge, i.e., the metal was drawn toward the extremities, leaving the greater thickness against the hinge. This feature was produced by hammering on an anvil. The holes in the butterfly hinge were never perfectly round because they were punched in by the blacksmith

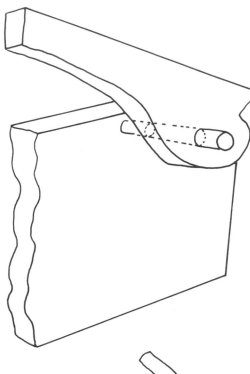

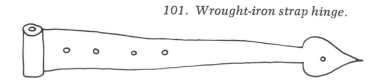

100. *Wooden pin hinge.*

101. *Wrought-iron strap hinge.*

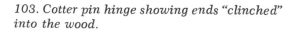

102. *Iron cotter pin hinge or staple hinge.*

103. *Cotter pin hinge showing ends "clinched" into the wood.*

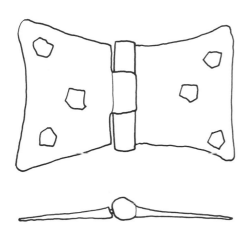

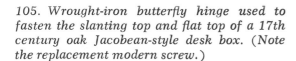

104. *Butterfly hinge.*

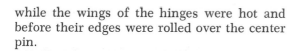

105. *Wrought-iron butterfly hinge used to fasten the slanting top and flat top of a 17th century oak Jacobean-style desk box. (Note the replacement modern screw.)*

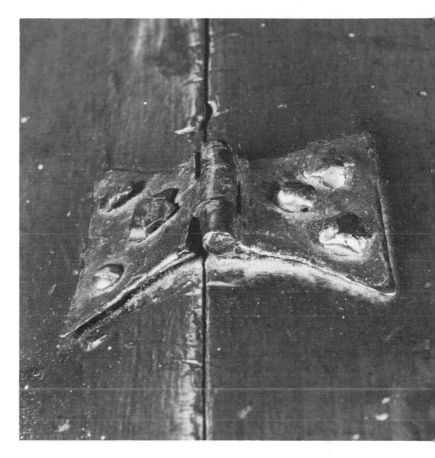

while the wings of the hinges were hot and before their edges were rolled over the center pin.

RECTANGULAR HINGES

Forms of rectangular hinges can be found used on furniture from the 17th century onward. The halves of the early hand-forged hinge are often of two thicknesses and slightly irregular. That is to say that a blacksmith has taken a thin strip of wrought iron, bent it double, and welded it together. The inner edge (the joint) is thus left rounded for the insertion of the pin which unites the two parts. A comparison of such an old hinge with a relatively modern one is made in illustration 106. Again, such hinges were usually attached with clinched nails or rivets.

The later machine-made iron hinge has leaves (or halves) stamped from a single thickness of metal, and the circular opening for the pin is evenly formed by curling one side of the leaf. The 18th century Dawes Cellarette shown here has an elaborately shaped hinge with part bent double surrounding the pin.

BRASS HINGES

Old brass hinges were made by hand-casting the leaves from molten metal. Slight imperfections in the shape and surface can therefore be determined. Modern ones are machine-stamped from sheets of rolled brass, bent to receive the iron hinge pin. Hence new brass hinges are much smoother and more even than the earlier cast ones, and certainly much stronger.

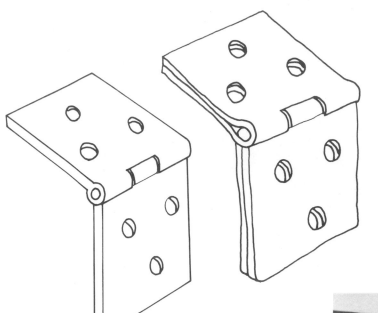

106. Modern rectangular iron hinge stamped from a single thickness of metal (left), and hand-wrought double-thickness iron hinge (right).

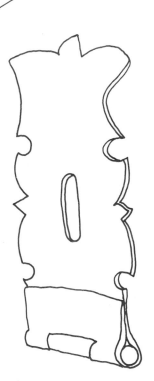

107. Elaborate iron hinge with end bent double.

108. Hinged late 18th century Continental cellarette which belonged to the patriot William Dawes, who rode with Paul Revere on the night of April 18, 1775.

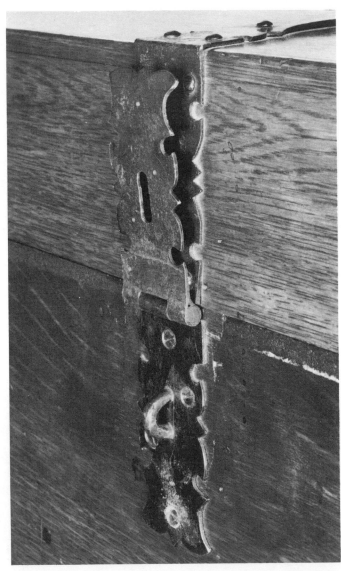

LOCKS

More than an accessory for decoration, locks have always served an important function as a means of security. Going back to the 14th century in Europe, chests were fitted with one or more hand-wrought iron locks. The movement (or works) of these early locks was sunken into the woodwork, and the faceplate was therefore flush with the surface of the chest. The hasp (the separate overlaid member) was hinged to its supporting metal strap, usually on the lid of the chest. Such hasp locks in their plain, rectangular form are common to chests and boxes of all periods.

Compact small brass locks for drawers of chests, cabinet doors, and the fall fronts of desks gradually evolved from the large, often highly complicated and elaborate iron locks used on medieval chests and other receptacles. In fact, few drawers in the 18th century were without locks. Again the works were embedded into the woodwork; a French or Continental lock mechanism was generally let into a slot in the front of the drawer whereas the usual English and American practice was to cut a plate for a lock so that the back of it lay flush with the back of the drawer front. (Note the two parts of the delicate lock embedded into the side and lid of the English dressing case in illustrations 211 and 212, page 173.) The lock is flush with the back edge of the lid side and the escutcheon plate here is missing, so that the keyhole is completely exposed. A covering decorative escutcheon plate (such as seen in illustration 110, page 85, or the drawer escutcheon plate in illustration 146, page 117) was placed over the keyhole on the front surface. The keyhole to the lock is simply outlined on the surface of the late 18th century drawer fronts with inlaid brass stringing (see illustration 8, page 19). During the mid-18th century, especially in France, the key sometimes served as a handle, no other handles being provided.

Sheraton in his *Cabinet Dictionary* of 1803 described the various kinds of locks used for cabinetwork accordingly:

"Of this useful instrument of security, there are various species. The common till lock, both spring and tumbler, used for drawers. The cupboard door kind, common, and spring and tumbler, used for bookcase and wardrobe doors. Box locks with link plates, such as for tea chests and wine cisterns. Mortice locks, some for doors, and others for sliders of cylindrical writing tables. Those for inner

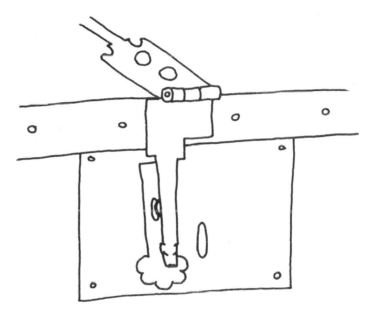

109. *Hand-wrought iron hasp lock, drawn from a 15th century European bridal casket.*

doors are called spring locks, and are the most considerable, both in use and structure. The principal parts of a spring lock are the main plate, the cover plate, and the pin hole; to the main plate belong the key hole, top hook, cross wards, bolt toe, draw back spring, tumbler, pin of the tumbler, and the staples; to the cover plate belong the pin, main ward, cross ward, step ward, or dap ward; to the pin hole belong the hook ward, main cross ward shank, the pot or broad bow ward and the bit."

Occasionally a lock is found stamped with a crown, the initial of the British reigning monarch, GR, WR, or VR, and the maker's name with the word "Patent" in capitals, a practice which began in the mid-19th century. The more important lock patentees included Bramah, Barron and Chubb. The maker's name was often omitted on early Victorian locks, however, and these were usually stamped with the crown and cypher and the words "Patent Secure Lever Lock," or something similar. Should one observe the marks of a file or emery wheel on either side of the levers, it is likely that the lock once had a Victorian name or patent which has been rubbed away to imply greater age.

BRASSES

Brasses, metal mounts made of brass, provide magnificent accent and decoration for a piece of furniture. At the same time they are useful as handles for drawers and doors or for the sides of heavy case pieces to accommodate lifting and carrying. Brasses must also be appreciated as a feat of remarkable craftsmanship and beauty in their own right. Styling is a most important consideration, and brasses have varied in style and material as the furniture itself has changed in style over periods of time.

Collectors in general take delight in examining a piece which still has its "original brasses," the brass mounts which were originally made or intended for the piece and the only ones it has ever had. However, this is not often the situation, as there are many reasons why the original brasses have, over the years, been removed and replaced. Changes in fashion would account for the disappearance of many, for owners wishing to be up to date would have the prevailing style fitted to furniture of an earlier date. The simple fact that brasses could be changed may well have tempted some owners to exchange their brasses for a later or earlier style of greater personal preference. In some other cases, original handles would get broken or become detached and lost due to natural wear and tear. Often an entire set of new brasses was fitted, this being less trouble than having one or two reproduced from those that remained.

When looking at a brass, immediate concern should be directed toward the encrustation which surrounds it. If this encrustation appears intact, i.e., the build-up of dirt, wax and dust around it appears undisturbed, there is good reason to believe that the brass is old and perhaps original to the piece. If an old brass is removed, the encrustation should contrast markedly with the exposed wood surface and the undisturbed wood beneath the brass. This undisturbed wood should appear quite beautiful due to the patina having developed without interruption. Encrustation can be recognized surrounding the escutcheon plate in illustration 110.

At the time the encrustation is being noted, doors and drawers should be examined for signs of having been fitted with other (and perhaps earlier) brasses. For example, on the drawer front there may be faint outlines of encrustation not matching the outline of the present brasses. (Outlines of earlier brasses may be detected despite refinishing because of the difference in patina resulting from the exposed and covered wood surfaces.) Another sign to look for is wooden plugs filling holes made by the bolts of earlier brasses. Examination of a piece's interior may reveal unexplained holes and other marks where different brasses were once attached. The pictured drawer interior is a typical sample of unqualified holes—and hence earlier brasses than the present.

In examining brasses, it should be kept in mind that all old brasses have a mellow surface patina which one comes to recognize with experience. The face of a 17th or 18th century brass is never completely smooth despite polishing, and this can be quickly ascertained by running one's finger across the face of several brasses in the same set. These old brasses have been cast by a craftsman and consequently slight variables caused by his hand and materials will be present. First, the designer or carver made the model, then the moulder made the mould and poured in the hot metal, and finally the chaser or fin-

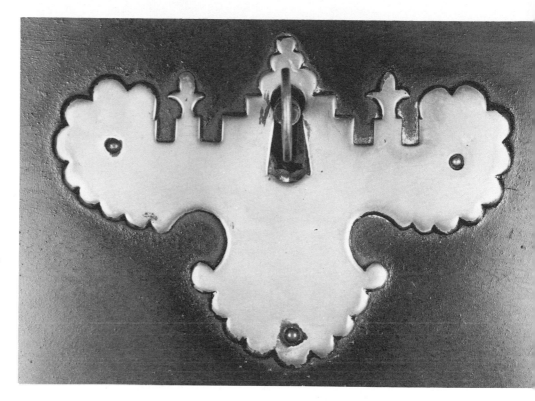

110. *Escutcheon plate surrounded by encrustation.*

isher cut away the faults in the casting, filed up the edges and polished the surfaces. The remaining subtle surface "waves," so delightful today, can be seen with the aid of a bright light, as well as felt. Other marks of hand craftsmanship (casting flaws, bubbles, etc.) can also be detected in this manner. Study the early brasses (illustrations 112 and 113). Queen Anne-style brasses which were engraved by hand with a set of punches will each be slightly different; the engraving will vary to a small extent from plate to plate and the plate outline is also likely to vary due to hand trimming and finishing.

The backside of the cast brass plate was not chased, finished, or polished, and it is

111. *Drawer with unqualified holes and marks inside the drawer front.*

112. Face of a mid-18th century hand-cast brass plate with its parts. Note slight imperfections due to hand craftsmanship.

therefore most important to examine this surface for the telltale signs of rough grain from the sand mould. It is again interesting to note that many seemingly flat brasses are, in fact, uneven on the front and on the back due to the early crude methods of production. (Modern reproduction plates are usually cut from sheet brass and are thus smooth and even on the back.)

PLATES AND PULLS

After consideration of the brass surfaces, the inside of the drawer should be explored to see how the brass has been attached to the drawer, this being of great significance in determining age. On early pieces that date from the late 17th century, the plates are flat, plain and thin. The small drop handles or pulls are fastened with a flat wire, called a tang, placed through a loop at the end of the pull, the two ends of the wire then being passed through a hole in the plate and the front of the drawer before being bent back on the drawer interior. Incidentally, the pear-shaped pulls found on doors and drawers of late 17th century furniture are invariably hollow or flat at the back; that is, they were only half the shape of the pear. This form remained in use for nearly a century, after which the whole pear shape was cast.

At the end of the 17th century an entirely new form of cabinet mount, the loop (or bail) handle with a flat shaped plate, often engraved and chamfer-edged, became the standard type and remained so throughout the first half of the 18th century. An example of this is the Queen Anne pull. The only connecting link between this new mount and its predecessor, the small drop, was the manner of fixing the handle to the plate by two iron or brass tangs. This double tang method, however, gave way to the use of a cast knob,

113. Rough backside of hand-cast brass plate.

a part of the back plate into which the ends of the loop handle were engaged (see drawing of bat wing brass, illustration 116). These knobs formed the face of the bolts whose cast square posts (or shanks) secured the back plate to the drawer by means of hand-filed threads and small, oddly shaped, rough cast metal nuts (see illustrations 116 and 117). (In reproductions, the bolts are round, the

90) follows this same simple shape. With the passing of the tang fixing, the loop was hung from the inner sides of the knobs and ornamented by a baluster-like detail in the center (see illustration 115). The baluster was later replaced with a plain heavy swelling, the ends of the handles curving inward.

A further use of the loop handle in this form developed after the publication of Chip-

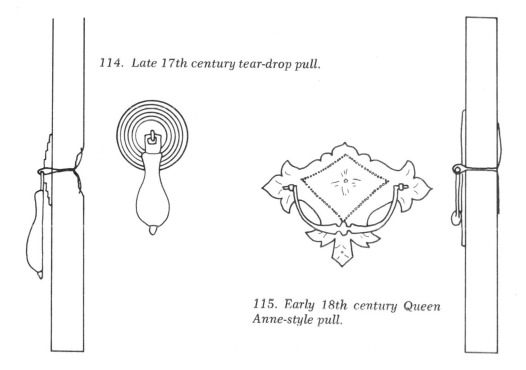

114. *Late 17th century tear-drop pull.*

115. *Early 18th century Queen Anne-style pull.*

threads are machined, and the nuts are larger and exactly square.) Old versus new nuts can be easily checked by inspecting the nuts on the inner side of the drawer where the posts come through from the front. Old nuts are cast as odd bits of brass tapped to fit loosely on the crude threads, and probably will fit only that particular post.

The loop handle also shows a rather distinct change in the first half of the 18th century. In its earliest form, the handle was thin, with the ends curving inward and ending in knobs which enabled them to be held in position by metal tangs. The wrought-iron handle on the hide trunk (illustration 121, page

pendale's *Director* in 1754 when the back plate was replaced by two small round or elliptical brasses made of cast brass with decorative grooved or beaded edges to which each end of the bail handle joined. The hole in the rosette plate was square, thus fitting the square shank of the bolt.

During the early 18th century the back plates, keyhole escutcheon plates, etc., were fixed to the drawer and door fronts with small round-headed brass pins. Screws were in use, but the proper equipment to make them sufficiently small for this use was lacking.

About 1780, back plates were no longer cast and engraved, nor ornamented with

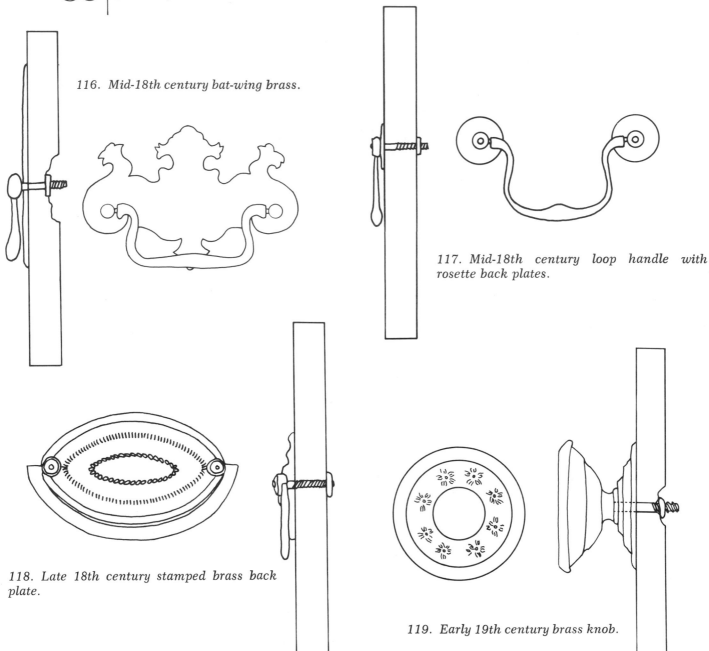

116. *Mid-18th century bat-wing brass.*

117. *Mid-18th century loop handle with rosette back plates.*

118. *Late 18th century stamped brass back plate.*

119. *Early 19th century brass knob.*

piercing, but instead made of thin rolled sheet brass stamped in relief. The bail handle became wider and hooked on to the post heads from the outside. (See drawing of Hepplewhite-style brass, illustration 118.) On fine delicate furniture, brasses or pulls of this type were sometimes of silver. Some metal back plates appearing between 1775 and 1800 were pressed into dies and the hollow at the back was filled in with composition. Pattern variety was great, including patriotic elliptical plates, geometric medallions, and symbolic designs of thistles, doves and conch shells. The diemakers of the period were skilled craftsmen producing sharply defined designs. It should be remembered that old posts were hand-cast, whereas reproductions are usually machine-turned from round stock.

Following the Hepplewhite- and Sheraton-style elliptical and rectangular shaped brasses, round brass knobs served as handles for drawers and doors. Again, they were usually stamped from sheet brass and filled with composition to add weight and strength. The screw was soldered directly to the knob, thereby eliminating separate posts. This unit held the backplate in position on the front and a nut screwed on the back held the brass knob secure to the wood (see illustration 119). Notice how the wood has been cut away directly around the screw at the back, thereby counter-sinking this detail and protecting it from activity in the drawer, at the same time protecting the contents of the drawer from damage by snagging.

Final observations in our consideration of brasses should include the importance given to chamfering the edges of these mounts. Stop-chamfering, or irregular cutting of the front surface edges, was also employed. (Often "cocks-head" hinges are found with stop-chamfering.) In the course of carefully scrutinizing sets of mounts to determine their age and place of origin, one often amusingly discovers that the cabinetmaker has had to "make do" with the brasses he had on hand for his current work. Naturally, he did not want to waste his existing supply and thus one occasionally finds much earlier style brasses used on a piece of furniture of far later style. Because brasses in Colonial America were primarily imported from England, what arrived was of course used—regardless of size and shape. Thus, for example, pieces of furniture in the Karolik Collection at the Museum of Fine Arts in Boston contains brasses which have been cut away or bent in order to fit into the available and planned area for each brass. So important a piece as the shell-carved Newport desk and bookcase (illustration 120) has imported "make-do" cut down and overlapping brasses on its fall front.

ORMOLU

Many brass and bronze mounts were gilded, particularly those in the mid-18th century rococo styles. This was done for additional beauty and to protect the metal against

120. "Make-do" brass on fall front of mahogany Goddard-Townsend School desk and bookcase, circa 1760–1775.

tarnishing. Work treated thus is called ormolu and the process was as follows: Mercury was heated in a crucible and, at the necessary temperature, pure gold was added. Upon forming an amalgam, the mixture was allowed to cool. The resulting paste was laid out on a flat surface and applied to the brass work with a wire brush, the article thus appearing to be painted silver. Washed and subjected to burning temperature, which caused the mercury to dissipate in fumes, the gold was left fast, ready for polishing or burnishing. The French, in particular, excelled in this technique.

IRON MOUNTS

Iron mounts have played a simple but important role in furniture history. Like the brass mounts, they perform the utilitarian function of handles for opening doors and drawers and for lifting and carrying pieces. They were usually ·hand-wrought, the work of the ordinary blacksmith. Hence they were simple hammered forgings with the occasional use of the punch, chisel and file for decoration and attempted smoothness. These straightforward mounts were intended for simple pieces of furniture such as country case furniture and utilitarian kitchen pieces (see illustration 121). The most elaborately decorated examples of wrought-iron mounts can be seen on medieval European chests and trunks.

Wrought-iron forgings were also used as braces or supports for parts of furniture where weakness was present or likely to occur. Therefore, supporting pieces of hand-wrought iron can be found anywhere on a piece. The early age of the iron piece is rec-

121. Simple hand-forged iron handle on a late 18th century hide trunk.

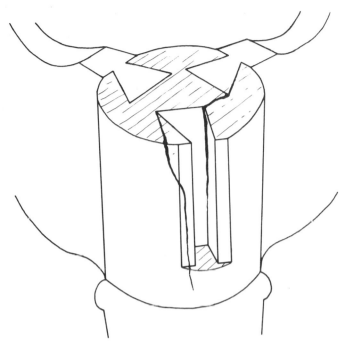

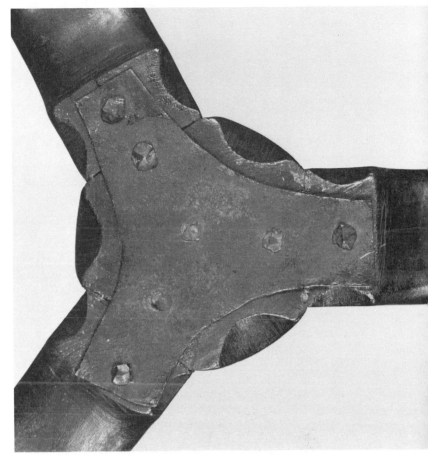

122. *Bottom of the central pedestal of a tripod table showing how the legs are slot-dovetail joined into the pedestal. Note the wood-splitting damage to the sides of the joint that occurs when downward pressure comes from the table top, producing side leverage.*

123. *Reinforcing hand-wrought iron plate found at the base of a tripod table pedestal.*

ognized by its uneven hammered surface, the shape of its outline, and the fact that it is attached with old nails or screws. Invariably, iron plates can be found under the pedestal of 18th century tripod tea tables, helping to support the joint where the three legs join the center pedestal. Any pressure on the table top is a threat to the three small legs being forced out of their joints, hence a reinforcing iron plate helps to keep them safely in place.

CASTORS

Small solid wheels attached to the lower extremities of a piece of furniture, enabling it to move without having to be lifted, seem to have been used in England as far back as the end of the 17th century. On the Continent they were used even earlier.

Early furniture incorporated hardwood wheels which were unable to swivel about a vertical axis. This shortcoming was remedied in the early 18th century when castors were introduced. They were secured into sockets with pins which allowed them to move in all directions, and early examples consisted of a boxwood ball running on a metal axle. This form was soon superseded by a boxwood roller. About 1750, leather castors came into use on high fashion furniture, a number of leather discs being strung together on the axle and held in position by brass "horns" attached to a flat metal plate. (The metal core fit up into the leg and was not visible.)

124. *A leather castor circa 1760* showing the leather "bowl" or wheel in three sections.

125. *Ceramic castor, mid-19th century English drop-leaf table.*

By 1770, castors made of brass (see illustration 32, page 30), with a socket type of fitting which encased the leg, were available in three styles, each in many stock sizes. Sheraton's *Cabinet Dictionary* illustrates several types of brass castor. He also lists five kinds of castors for bed posts. In Regency period tables the socket (or bucket) often takes the form of a lion's paw foot of brass or the surfaces are decorated with honeysuckle, acanthus or other designs in relief, some of these paw castors contain several wheels. During the Victorian years, white ceramic castors were produced and successfully used on chairs and small tables.

GLASS

Glass, particularly in the form of secretary door glasses and looking glasses, is a most important factor in establishing the authenticity of old furniture. It was well into the latter part of the 19th century before the art of making perfectly flat sheet glass in large sizes was developed.

With its many imperfections, 18th century glass is easily identifiable. Anyone with the good fortune to possess examples, whether in the form of a looking glass, windows in a house, or as part of a piece of furniture, should treat them with great care. Old glass is extremely brittle! Due to methods of manufacture (blowing and casting), old glass is of unequal thickness, never truly flat and often curved. These characteristics provide a pleasing play of light on the panes, though there is some distortion of objects seen through the glass. This unevenness (bumpiness, imperfections and occasional air bubbles) can actually be felt. Old glass will always have a greenish, bluish or brownish color cast.

Looking glasses of polished metal or silvered glass have been highly prized from very early times. Small looking glasses, chiefly from Venice, were imported into England early in the 15th century. The making of silvered glass became an established industry in England during the reign of William and Mary (1689–1702) and heavy duties on glass were imposed in 1695. These duties affected the United States as an English colony by severely curtailing the use of glass in secretary doors and other furniture—as well as for architectural purposes. (Windows were few and small until after the Revolution.)

Glass plates of any size were very expensive to make, and the best were generally imperfect. The old silvering for looking glasses was done by the mercury process,

126. Early 19th century breakfront secretary door of contemporary glass panes. Note the imperfections in the glass.

127. Arrangement for setting the individual panes of glass into the molding tracery of a glazed secretary door. Each pane, cut to the appropriate shape, is positioned against the backside of the astragal molding and held in place with putty.

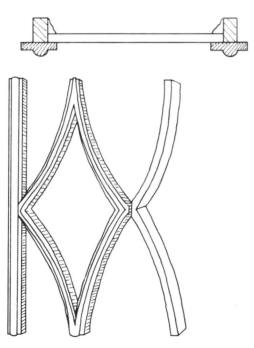

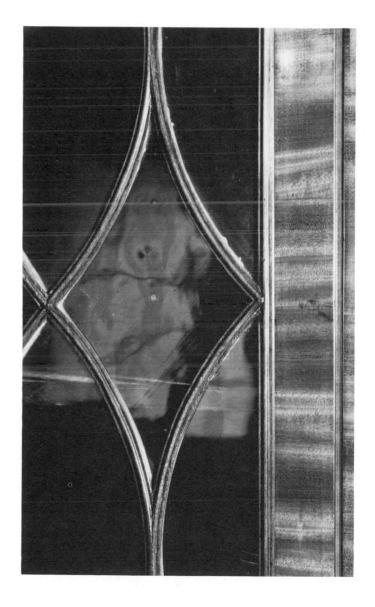

where quicksilver was "floated" on the back of glass, adhering only by its cohesion with a perfect surface. Quicksilver, being heavy, would be liable to fall off if the glass had any irregularities (and old glass is rarely perfect), so that today the silvering on old looking glasses is always spotted, fogged or missing in several areas. In addition, as the mercury is on the back, any discoloration of the glass itself was noticeable on the front; 18th century glass nearly always has a bluish tinge.

Today the silvering of mirrors is done by the "patent" process, with silver foil used in place of mercury. A good test for an old looking glass, even if it has been resilvered (and by the "patent" method) is to hold up a sheet of white paper to it and observe the reflection—the blue tint of the old glass becomes apparent at once.

Truly old silvered glass remains difficult to detect, however, as the mercury process is still done on fakes. When mercury is applied to glass with an uneven back, it will soon fog and spot. The old bevels are also carefully imitated. Both the genuine and the fake bevels differ from the modern in being very broad and shallow with a very subtle demarcation line between the bevel and the face of the glass, almost as if they had been molded with the glass instead of being ground with a sand-wheel. Bevelled glass is characteristic of Queen Anne period looking glasses and its flatness is due in part to the great thinness of the glass at that time.

9

FINISH

FINISH ON A PIECE of furniture is often loosely described as its patina. All finishes have patinas, and all patinas are to some extent the product of the furniture finishes. However, the two words are not synonymous.

PATINA

"Patina" is a word used to describe a particular old furniture surface condition, a soft, warm, mellow look which comes with age and circumstances. The quality of furniture patina depends upon the care a piece has received, its situation and the conditions to which it has been exposed during its lifetime.

The purest definition of patina would be the act of simple oxidation of raw wood over time. This alone, without the addition of such outside elements as stain, wax and dirt, will give wood a "smoked" color and tone. The rafters in an old barn serve as a case in point. Once the barn has been completed, the rafters remain untouched. Yet fifty or a hundred years later, they will appear "smoky" and weathered as the result of oxidation, the wood's interaction with the atmosphere. Secondary surfaces on pieces of furniture will have this same look—the bottoms of drawers and the backs of case pieces, for example. This "old" look is in obvious contrast to the looks and feel of a new piece of wood and it is virtually impossible to imitate.

The word patina is usually *not* used in reference to secondary wood surfaces on furniture, but is reserved for primary surfaces. In addition to undergoing the process of normal oxidation, a primary furniture surface has likely been stained and possibly treated with some finish as well. Over time, this surface has been waxed, rubbed (causing gentle friction), oiled, polished, dirtied, worn and at times inadvertently allowed to fade from exposure through a sunny window. The handsome result is what is commonly meant by the word patina.

True patina is by far the most beautiful and appealing single feature found in an old piece of furniture. It is impossible to reproduce, although attempts are made. After careful examination of true patinated surfaces, and a basic knowledge of the typical old finishes and their behavior over time, one can usually detect questionable patina.

KINDS OF FINISH

Finishing treatments have always been used on furniture and these so-called "finishes," each with its own characteristics, strengths and weaknesses, have served as a

128. *Door of an early 17th century cupboard from Darcarlia, Sweden. The brightly colored painting is dated 1813.*

protection and preservative to the piece of furniture. The beauty of the piece—its wood figure, its proportions, its decorative detail—have all been enhanced with the application of one or more finishes to its primary surfaces.

Obviously, many things are likely to have happened to a piece of furniture over its history. Since surface finish is highly vulnerable to change and damage, this makes determining original finish or the history of a piece's finish extremely challenging. One could easily find that an 18th century piece which was originally oiled and subsequently waxed

had been French Polished later and, afterwards rewaxed. Sometimes only parts have been treated in this way—a badly marked table top may have been stripped down and French Polished, for instance, and the remainder left untouched. Most varnished and shellacked 18th century pieces have very likely been refinished several times since they were made.

PAINT

A simple kind of finish and one easily accessible to all cabinetmakers was milk paint. (Sour milk and rust provided a red color, for example.) This proved an attractive and protective finish with such colorful results as green or black Windsor chairs and painted, decorated, Pennsylvania Dutch chests. Sometimes they were most extravagant in their painted detail—as in the 17th century Swedish cupboard pictured here—which was painted in 1813. Paint covered up any imperfections in the wood, such as knotholes. (In fact, if a piece were made of pine, it was usually painted.) Paint as a finish also disguised the cabinetmaker's use of several woods in the same piece of furniture (again the Windsor chair comes to mind), and it proved to be indeed durable as verified by the many early pieces extant today (even allowing for the current fashion of stripping such pieces and refinishing with varnish or shellac).

The approximate age of paint can be established. Old paint, 100 years or older, is tenacious. It is brittle and extremely difficult to remove. This is because over time oxidation has taken place and the natural oils in the paint have evaporated. Consequently, a quick test for age is to scratch the paint surface with a knife. The paint will shatter if old. However, if it is new and still contains its natural oils, it will roll off in curls much like the curled shavings from a plane.

VARNISH

Varnish is a strong finish used on all types and most styles of furniture. Generally it is water and alcohol resistant and thus a very durable and practical finish. The shortcoming of varnish is the opaque hairline checking, sometimes called "alligatoring" because of its crackle appearance, which occurs in the course of time (see illustration 41, page 37). Although the presence of alligatoring is an excellent indication that the varnish finish is indeed old, it obscures the figure and color of the wood, giving the piece a cold, dull appearance.

A test of an old varnish is to rub a small surface area with sandpaper. Because the natural oils will have dried (oxidized) in old varnish, the finish will powder when sanded. In contrast, a very new varnish finish will roll off in curls when sanded because little oxidation has taken place.

A further test for determining a varnish finish (as opposed to shellac, for example) is to apply a small amount of alcohol to an obscure area of the finish. If the finish does

129. *Tall clock case providing a dramatic example of "alligatored" old varnish.*

not react (i.e., if it withstands the alcohol), it is very likely that the piece has been finished in varnish, not in shellac.

SHELLAC

Shellac is the hardest and most durable organic finish. Shellac gums are derived from the exudation of the lac insect (an aphid) which lives on the twigs of certain trees. These gums are cut (mixed) with alcohol to form a ready-to-use finish. The most resilient of all finishes, shellac will take much abuse and wear. It is also the most challenging finish to properly apply to a furniture surface, as it must be laid on perfectly (correct quantity in the correct places) the first time. Problems with brush strokes, bubbles, etc., can only be corrected by sanding off that coat and redoing it. Since it dries quickly the finisher must also work with speed. Shellac is applied with a brush or by the French Polish method using a cloth pad. The end result is unrivalled for its beauty, luster, and sheen when rubbed by hand. One cabinetmaker who works frequently with both varnish and shellac likens varnish to maple syrup, and shellac to whipped cream.

Shellac is likely to be the finish used on all important dark wood pieces of furniture, especially during the 18th century. (Its use goes back at least to the 1600's.) However, since shellac is vulnerable to heat, water and alcohol, shellacked furniture must receive care and protection.

The sandpaper test will show the age of a shellac finish. An old finish will turn to a yellowish powder on the sandpaper. This is because the alcohol has evaporated during the course of time—leaving only the resin or shellac gums. Newly mixed and applied shellac when sanded will gum the paper, since not enough time has elapsed for the alcohol to evaporate out.

The alcohol test described on page 97 is an effective method of determining whether a surface has been treated with shellac or varnish. Once again, such testing should always be done on an unimportant area.

OIL

The oiled finish simply involves repeated applications of oil to the raw wood surface which soon produces a finished look and some protection for the wood. The use of this finish is more characteristic of modern furniture than of antique period pieces.

STAIN

Another straightforward method of finishing a piece was to stain it and then follow this with a coat of beeswax and turpentine. Stains are preparations which are thinner than paint and are thus absorbed by wood pores without forming a coating. Early stains provide interesting study, as almost anything was used—berries, animal urine, walnut extract made from boiling walnut shells, syrups, dragon's blood made from tree bark, ground roots and chemicals (sulphuric acid, vinegar, ammonia, copper sulfate, coal tar, etc.). Tea was an especially good dye for oak. If a chemical stain has been used on the wood, the wood will *never* fade in sunlight; if anything, it will get darker. Hence, some early mahogany chairs are almost black. Contrarily, if the stain is organic or natural (derived from animals or plants), it will fade with sun exposure and time. This latter effect is the most desirable by today's standards of beautiful patina.

END GRAIN FINISH

End grain wood, the result of cuts made perpendicular to the wood grain, takes on a special finish which is clearly visible to the eye. When finish is applied to the ends of cut boards used in furniture construction, these ends will absorb more stain than the surrounding wood and, therefore, appear darker. This is because end grain contains more open tracheid vessels, or pores, with which to absorb the stain.

Although end grain appears in its most obvious form at the end of a cut board, every cut into any board will expose some amount of end grain. All carving, for example, involves end grain exposure and thus the variation in stain absorption is explained, i.e., rather than dust and dirt collecting in the corners of a typical carving and making it seem darker (although this may be partly true, of course), these cut-in areas are areas of end grain exposure and consequently have absorbed a larger amount of stain. The ball-

and-claw foot is an example of the exposure of end grain. The corners between the claws and the top of the ball are end grain surfaces and hence will always appear darker, again because of the extra stain absorption due to more tracheid vessels opened with wood cut in this direction (see illustration 40, page 36).

Attempts are made to even the stain between end grain and regular grain by fewer applications to end grain surfaces or use of a diluted stain on such areas, but total success is almost impossible. Note the variation in color on the photographed cabriole leg. The top side of the pad foot, having greater end grain exposure, is darker. The top side of the knee is also darker for the same reason. The turned legs of a Sheraton side chair or early New England slat-back chair owe much of their lovely surface interest to the varied absorption rate of stain, again the intermittent end grain surfaces absorbing greater quantities and thus appearing darker. End grain table edges also prove this point.

End grain should not be confused with "open grain." Open grain has a rather strict meaning and is used in reference to old versus new wood. When a piece of mahogany, for example, is freshly cut, the pores (grain) will appear open. In contrast, due to age and applied finish, the grain of an old piece of mahogany will appear closed. Immediately, my grandmother's kitchen table comes to mind. This old table has been rubbed, waxed and even refinished so many times that the grain is totally closed (pores and vessels filled), giving the wood a metallic appearance. This effect must be seen to be truly appreciated. Good examples of smooth closed grain can be found on the bottoms of chair and stool feet, such as the one here shown.

In judging the authenticity of an "antique" it is helpful to remember that open grain wood is never found on genuine old pieces. The pores of such pieces have long

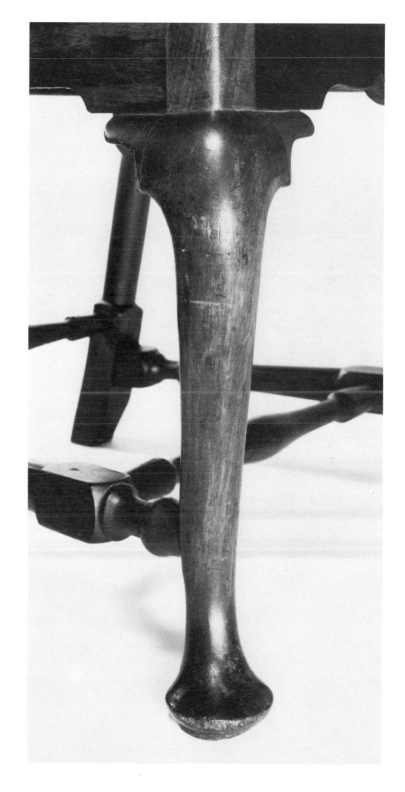

130. Cabriole leg showing color variation due to end grain exposure.

and glue, to name a few. An ordinary finishing treatment required many coats to conquer the "valleys" of the open grain. As each coat of shellac or varnish filled in some of the valley, the new height added to the "mountain" would be sanded down. Coats of finish would be applied and treated in this manner until the valley floors were level with the sanded mountain tops, thereby producing a lovely smooth surface.

GILDING

Gilding is a finishing process applied to furniture which dates back to the days of the ancient Egyptian Pharaohs. As early as 3000 B.C., the discovery had been made that the extreme malleability of gold allowed it to be beaten into a skin so thin that it would adhere to a preparation of plaster. In Europe since the Middle Ages, two distinct methods of overlaying wood with gold leaf have been used, oil-gilding and water-gilding.

Oil-gilding. This is a process in which the final application is a preparation of "gold size" (boiled oil) to which the gold adheres. It has the advantage of rendering the gilded surface partly waterproof, but the gold cannot be highly toned or burnished (it would rub off), thus lacking the luster of good water-gilding. It is quite doubtful that the oil-gilding process was ever applied to furniture in the 18th century; it was used for outside work such as the gilding of signs and weathervanes.

Water-gilding. Gilding of this type is always applied on a carefully prepared and smoothed gesso and/or red clay ground applied over the wood. (Although a gesso ground is often used for oil-gilding too, one of the advantages of oil-gilding is that it can be done on a ground less laborious to prepare.) When water-gilding was planned for a piece, the wood carving was frequently left incomplete, such delicate details as veining being left to the gilder, who cut them into the gesso ground using pointed sticks and water in his final preparation. Thus, to strip an old looking glass frame to the bare wood, for example, is to destroy much of the finer detail.

131. *Example of smooth closed grain as observed on the bottom of the ball-and-claw foot.*

since been closed up with repeated applications of finish, dirt, wax and the effects of wear.

As mentioned earlier, the grain or pores of some woods are naturally larger than those of others, regardless of age or quantity of applied finish. Ash, oak and walnut are woods with unusually large, open pores. Such pores always mean a "valley and mountain" uneven raw wood surface which requires filling to achieve a smooth surface. During the 18th and 19th centuries, pores of open-grained woods were sometimes filled with "fillers"—scraping varnish, whiting, plaster of paris

Old gilding simply looks old. All fakery attempts to duplicate this old appearance, and thus all gilding should be studied carefully for appropriate signs. The gilding should show signs of wear and tear, perhaps exposing evidence of old gesso ground. It will contain a number of flecks, checks and marks, often due to loosening gesso ground. The gilded surface will also appear darkened. New flecks and checks are visually very different from those that are old and mellowed; and thus identifiable. Pictured here is the gilded handrest of a French fauteuil armchair whose badly chipped old gilding reveals the core wood and gesso coating underneath. A test for gold is the use of nitric acid, which will

132. *Detail of old gilding. Note hairline cracks and general feeling of age.*

133. *Late 18th century watergilded highly-styled looking glass (see detail, illustration 132).*

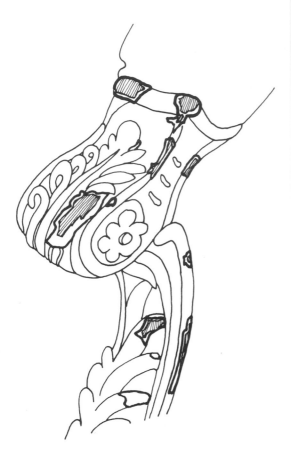

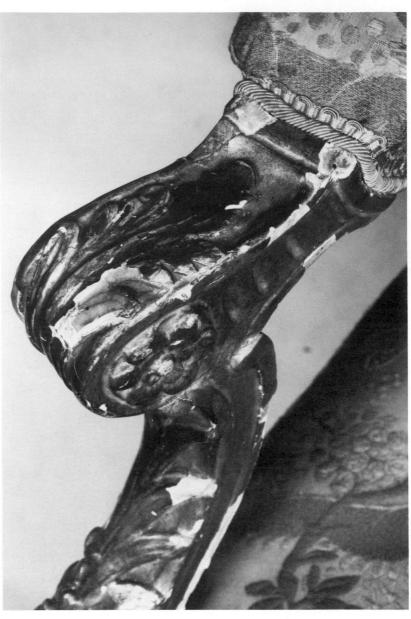

134. Hand rest of an 18th century armchair showing core wood and gesso coating under the gilded surface. Visibly layered areas are clarified in the drawing.

quickly turn green any gold alloy of less than 9 carats.

LACQUER AND JAPANNING

These are two very distinct furniture finishes quite similar in design—the japanning technique in fact having been developed to imitate the true Asiatic lacquering. Eastern lacquer artisans started with even grain pine wood which they primed with sticky lacquer. Hemp cloth or silk was then pressed on to form a base. Twenty-four hours later the surface was hard enough to be polished smooth with whetstone, and another coat of lacquer was applied. This lacquer process was repeated twenty to thirty times—with each application carefully brushed on—not too slowly for fear the lacquer would dry too hard and not too quickly lest it not be smooth or hard enough. The Rhus Verniciflua or "lac tree," whose sap is the basic ingredient of lacquer, is grown only in China, Japan and Malaya, thus Europeans were forced to resort to an imitation method appropriately termed "japanning" in the late 17th century.

In the *Handmaid to The Arts* (1758) Robert Dassie writes that "by japanning is to be understood the art of covering bodies by grounds of opake (sic) colours in varnish; which may be either afterwards decorated by painting or gilding, or left in a plain state." The wood, first treated with a mixture of whitening and size, was then coated with two or more applications of varnish composed of gum-lac, seed-lac or shellac, and dissolved in spirits of wine with other gums and substances also being employed. Black, tortoise shell and red were the normal base colors. Raised gesso decoration was used on all important pieces. American colonial japanners working in Boston and New York, the two centers for this craft between 1720 and 1750, simplified the English method by using fine-grained woods for their case pieces, thereby eliminating the need for a gesso-like base on the wood surfaces. They also did away with

135. Detail, japanned high chest of drawers, circa 1745, with original finish. How splendid it must have been in its high-gloss newly finished state.

the costly and time-consuming mixing of seed-lac varnish with ground colors by simply applying clear varnish over the coats of paint.

The difference between lacquer and japanning techniques becomes obvious when they are compared. Indications of original finish would be the same as those mentioned already for a varnish finish and gilding. Most examples of lacquer have suffered with age, particularly the softer japanned pieces. Scratches, dents, cracks and chips are frequent, as shown in the close-up photo of the original japanned finish on a Boston circa 1745 high chest of drawers. Japanned pieces have also often been coated, probably for protection, with thick opaque varnish which sometimes hides the entire design.

DATING A FINISH

Besides the methods mentioned above, there are additional tests for assessing the age of a finish. One of these is the evidence to be found by removing a drawer pull or other piece of hardware. The "finish" under a pull, although probably cleaner, or different,

should nevertheless give an impression consistent with the age of the surrounding wood as in illustration 136. The presence of drip marks may suggest the hasty work of today's finisher, particularly if the drips do not pass the finish tests of age or do not blend or relate to the obvious age of the piece. This is not to say that drip marks made by earlier craftsmen cannot be found, but these drips will comply with quick age tests and, more important, will harmonize with their surround.

The use of ultraviolet radiation is an interesting modern technique which is helpful in providing surface finish information. Newly-cut, unfinished wood floresces very little; the florescence of old wood is largely due to the surface patina it has received through the years. Old furniture thus produces some florescence due to surface treatment. New varnish, for example, floresces a bright violet, while old wood with aged patina floresces a whitish color. Although florescence alone cannot be used to tell the difference between old and new work, it can reveal additions and alterations more dramatically and effectively than sunlight.

136. Comparison of surface finish under and around drawer pull. Note how the outline of the brass (encrustation) is absorbed into both areas of finish.

10

VENEER AND MARQUETRY

VENEER

Veneering is a form of construction and decoration which dates back to ancient Egypt. Veneer work was extensively produced during the 17th, 18th and 19th centuries and still is done to decorate furniture surfaces by using rare and richly figured woods, often combined in patterns. See the delicate, intricate veneer arrangements in the photographed late 18th century New England card table (illustration 137). Veneering—covering the surface of a comparatively common wood with a thin glued skin of another more exotic and expensive wood—also makes it possible to obtain the greatest use of special rare woods. Wood of a twisty or odd nature (such as walnut burls), which would be too unstable for constructional use in the solid, could be successfully used as thin slices of interesting veneer. As all pieces of a stack of veneers from one piece of wood (known as a flitch or parcel in the trade) are identical, this reality can be exploited by piecing them together in a variety. of ways producing matching patterns impossible to obtain with solid wood. (See the matched crotch mahogany veneered drawer fronts in illustration 8, page 19.) Veneer stringing, narrow long veneer pieces set into the veneered wood, is often a part of these patterns, and character-

istic of 17th century banded or string veneer work are the different timber veneers on each side of this line of detail. Sometimes when the veneer background is continuous, often a characteristic of late 18th century pieces, the stringing is a later embellishment.

Furniture cores intended for veneer overlay were usually of fine quality pine (and in England, deal) during the 18th century. (Any core wood imperfection would ultimately effect the surface veneer.) Oak was similarly used, particularly for walnut and the more expensive early mahogany veneered furniture. After 1750, Honduras mahogany was sometimes used as a ground for veneer. The process of laying down a sheet of veneer required great skill and care on the part of the craftsman. The veneer was applied to the core wood with hot glue, then weighted in place with cauls (or sandbags when the surface curved) and heavy clamping. When the glue became dry the surface was smoothed, planed, sanded and finished.

Before the introduction of machinery, veneer was cut with a hand-saw and measured from a sixteenth to an eighth of an inch thick. The thickness of early veneer is apparent in illustration 139 which shows a damaged veneer surface on an English mid-18th century secretary-bookcase. Now that it is prepared by machinery, veneer is rarely more than a thirty-second of an inch thick

137. *Late 18th century New England Hepplewhite-style card table of elaborate veneered patterns in contrasting dark and light woods. The curly-figure rectangular front panels are likely to be birch, which is often mistaken for satinwood.*

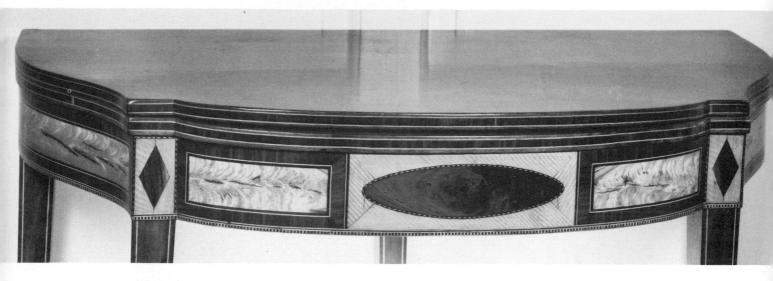

138. *Burl walnut veneered top surface of an early 18th century dressing table. Burl veneer is characteristically quartered or applied in four sections as such a large piece of burl would not be obtainable. The veneered burl walnut center is surrounded with herringbone veneer stringing and plain-figure walnut cross-banded veneer.*

and often less than a sixtieth. This is helpful to know in the detection of fake pieces. It is also one of the reasons why modern veneer holds better than the old hand-cut material, for glue will hold a thin sheet better than a thick one.

In the 19th century a machine was introduced to cut veneers with a knife, slicing it in layers of any thickness required. This remains the modern practice and is carried out in two ways. The first is to slide the log in the same way as saw-cut boards, thus producing "slice veneer" which contains figure similar to that found in old saw-cut veneers. The second is to mount the log in a form of lathe known as a peeler. As the log revolves, a knife is advanced against it, peeling off a continuous band until the whole of the log, except the center, has been cut. This rotary-cut veneer is the width of the trunk's length, thin and absolutely without figure.

There are several other intricacies in veneer cutting which are worthy of note. One of these is the cleaving of burl veneers from the boles of old walnut trees (see page 23). The merchant who trades in fancy veneers is always on the lookout for freak growths, and trees which have been polled offer many varieties. Polled olive, elm, walnut and ash, for example, yield handsome veneers, although only in small, brittle pieces. As seen in illustration 8, page 19, "crotch mahogany," cut from a tree crotch and split to produce the desirable plume figure was handsomely exploited by cabinetmakers from the mid-18th century onward. Another refinement was the cutting of saplings and branches transversely into "oyster pieces" (see page 22). Laburnum, with its yellow sap-ring and dark heart-produced handsome examples of this technique, and almond, walnut and kingwood were among the other timbers utilized in this manner.

MARQUETRY

Marquetry is a kind of veneer, a composite of pieces of veneer arranged in elaborate floral patterns and arabesques forming a thin panel which is glued to the core wood.

139. Damaged mahogany veneer surface.

Veneered marquetry was a Dutch craft brought to England in a fully developed state about 1670. It flourished until 1715, especially as ornamentation for tall clock cases, and was again revived by Chippendale and his contemporaries during the late 1760's, using the delicate motifs of the neo-classic style. The laying of veneers in scrolls and foliated patterns worked in brass and ebonized wood again came into favor in the Regency period of the early 1800's. Marquetry was also introduced into France from Holland, again in the late 17th century, where it never lost interest or appeal, especially in the urbane court circle of Paris during the 18th century.

The design of early marquetry copied from the Dutch was floral, depicting flowers in vases with birds and utilizing many woods. The "seaweed" variety of marquetry has a pattern representing flowing lines of seaweed

139A. French drop-front secretary of veneered marquetry with ormolu mounts made by Jean-Henri Riesner (1734–1806) for Queen Marie Antoinette in 1790. Riesner's signature appears at the bottom right of the lower marquetry panel. Photograph courtesy The Frick Collection.

139B. *Detail of the Riesner secretary central panel showing the varieties of wood used in the marquetry work and the richly sculptured gilded bronze ornaments. Photograph courtesy The Frick Collection.*

and involved only one wood to contrast with the ground; it also resembles the finer leaves of the endive plant and thus is occasionally described as "endive marquetry." The "arabesque" variety, in wood with a flowing scroll design, was inspired by the brass and tortoiseshell marquetry designs of the French royal cabinetmaker (ébéniste du roi), André-Charles Boulle (1642–1732). Unique and famous to Boulle was his method of preparing his decorative marquetry panels: sheets of brass and tortoiseshell were glued together and then cut with a saw to the desired pattern. When cut, the layers were separated and then combined to provide one panel of tortoiseshell ground inlaid with brass and one of brass inlaid with shell, known as "first part" and "counter part." A pair of commodes, therefore, might be veneered, one with first part Boulle marquetry and the other with counter part Boulle work.

In all types of English marquetry the pattern was usually formed by fitting light-colored woods into darker background woods such as walnut, coromandel or lignum vitae. However, French and Continental marquetry represented endless variety in its exquisite design, detail and form. The entire marquetry process was done with a fine saw, thereby providing the scope for elaborate designs. That is to say that the veneers of the design were cut and composed into a panel before the panel was glued to the core—veneer being thin it could be cut with a saw before application instead of the core wood having to be laboriously chopped away with a chisel to receive the inlay. The many parts to a particular design were each cut separately by the extremely skilled marquetry cutter and they made a perfect fit, one within the other. As the parts were cut they were assembled on a flat tray and paper was glued over the whole to hold it together until final application.

Some marquetry was shaded—especially the green stained holly wood leaves of flowers. This was done by dipping one end of the piece (or leaf) of veneer into hot sand so that it became slightly scorched. The inlaid light wood urns on the legs of the drop-leaf table (illustration 160, page 127) have sand-scorched details. Such shading was permanent and could be controlled by the amount of time the wood was immersed and the extent of veneer covered by the sand. The veins of leaves or the petals of a flower, when made of one piece of veneer, were produced by saw cuts which were then filled with dark colored wax to accentuate them. Much of this subtle detail is lost when the piece is refinished—an indication, incidentally, that the piece *has* been refinished.

PARQUETRY

Parquetry is a variation of the marquetry veneer technique, contemporary with the late 17th century marquetry fashion, in which the veneer pieces of wood were carefully fitted together in repeating geometric patterns. An English Carolean-style cabinet-on-stand, circa 1685, with veneered oysterpieces and cross-cuttings of geometric diamonds made of contrasting walnut veneer would be an example of this type of decorative work.

The most elaborate examples of parquetry veneer are to be found on 18th century French pieces. Not only have subtle variations of color been echoed back and forth by geometric diaper (repeating) pattern parquetry but the detail work is pointed up and framed (thus protected) with bronze doré (gilded bronze) mounts and moldings held in place with screws. Close examination of such superb marquetry pieces of furniture should always reveal carefully chosen, matched veneers and finely drawn and cut marquetry parts. It should be remembered that the Paris and provincial guilds of marqueteurs demanded a high standard of craftsmanship from their members, and that a master ébéniste would not permit any work to leave his shop which did not come up to these standards. Thus any piece exhibiting poorly done marquetry work becomes highly suspect.

PART

II

WHAT HAPPENS TO FURNITURE WITH TIME

CHAPTER

11

POINTS OF WEAR

WEAR, SUCH A universal happening caused by time and use, plays an informative role in the analysis of potentially old and therefore "antique" furniture. It will be realized, as we explore the many things that happen to furniture over time, that wear is only one consideration. However, it becomes a most obvious and readily identifiable factor once serious searching begins. Signs of wear serve as good evidence that the piece has been used for a long time, thus quite naturally having marks of wear. This is certainly some proof that the piece is old.

The search for signs of wear is a matter of common sense, since wear will be the result of how and where the piece of furniture is or was used. Wear will not be evenly located everywhere on a piece; every "moveable" (piece of furniture) has some parts which are subject to particular stress and others which receive frequent handling. These areas will show the greatest signs of wear.

TABLES AND CHAIRS

Many signs and degrees of wear can be observed in studying a table. These will vary according to the purpose and use of the table but will be there. Signs to look for include an uneven table top surface, smoothed and/or

irregular edges, and scratches. The corners on an old table are likely to be nicked and bruised where chairs have knocked against them. If the table has a trestle base, this will no doubt show the wearing down and markings of many shoes having rested there in the past. Table legs and feet too, will show signs of use from marred by chairs and cleaning implements, as well as being used as resting spots for shoes. Sometimes the feet of a table will be almost entirely worn away. This is often true for early examples of butterfly, gateleg and tavern tables with their small turned button or knob feet.

An old chair is also likely to have many points of wear. The first point might be at the top of the back, where a hand has probably clutched the chair untold times to bring it to the table. Consequently, the top rail will be smooth and worn. Again, the back is likely to show signs of having been pushed up against the wall, and of people leaning it against the wall while sitting on it. Further proof of this habit is often evidenced by the uneven wear on the wall-side of ladderback chair finials (see illustration 141).

Because chairs are frequently dragged from area to area in the line of use, the legs over time will show many signs of abuse and wear. (See illustration 124, page 92.) Typically, the outer sides of the front and back legs (or feet if the chair has them) will be

113

140. *Five-banister-back New England armchair, circa 1700–1720*

141. *Backs of the ball-and-button finials on banister-back chair showing extensive wear from use.*

bruised and sometimes smoothed or even partially worn away. (See illustration 130, page 99.) In some cases, the feet will have completely disappeared. The base of feet, when closely studied, will appear to have a hard polish often scored by fine lines where, over time, particles of grit have been trapped between the wood and the floor surface. (See the bottom of the ball-and-claw foot, illustration 131, page 100.) Edge wear can sometimes be confirmed by tilting and dragging an old chair and comparing where the wear should appropriately be and where in fact it is.

Among the most charming points of wear on a chair are the uneven stretchers. These will often be partially worn (and thus uneven) from use as resting spots for shoes. The wear will be found to be deeper on the outside than on the inside edge of the stretcher, and the line of wear will tend to be fairly regular, as the foot did not always rest in exactly the same spot. On a spurious piece, however, the appearance of wear will usually be quite uneven and wear marks will be as deep on the inside of the stretcher as on the outside.

Chair arms and hand rests will sometimes

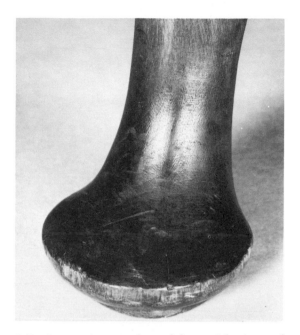

142. *Queen Anne-style pad foot with signs of use and wear on the toe.*

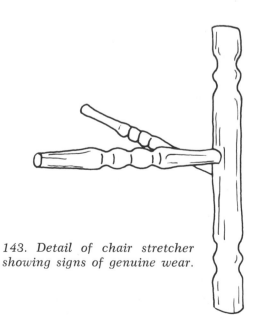

143. *Detail of chair stretcher showing signs of genuine wear.*

144. *Turned front stretchers on a child's high chair well-worn by children's feet.*

show similar signs of wear. Note the detail photograph of a "carver" chair (illustration 145.) Child versions of these Pilgrim-type chairs will often reveal that the backsides of the back posts have been worn flat from top to foot. The reason might seem mysterious until one lays the chair on its back on the floor. The whole back post rests flatly on the floor and the upturned chair seat is just the right height for a toddling one-year-old child. A good guess might consequently be that such a chair was used as a "walker," and this

wear on the chair posts is due to the child pushing the chair about on the floor. The banister-back chair in illustration 141 shows wear on its posts, along with the finials, suggesting that it, too, has been used as a walker.

CASE PIECES

With case pieces many of the same points of wear and use are in evidence. Bracket or ball-and-claw feet of a chest of drawers or a secretary-bookcase, for example, will show signs of wear from being knocked against; part of a foot may be worn or broken away from being moved or dragged about; and any number of bangs, dents, marks and stains will be noticeable everywhere. Old clock cases are frequently damaged to some extent at their base by brooms and other objects and by the impact of feet during winding. Although this latter point of wear is rarely noticed, observation will bear it out. With some clock cases, a protective strip of wood, appropriately called a kick-plate, is added to the bottom of the case.

The drawers of a case piece are an excellent source for signs of wear. The face of the drawer will show the signs of use one might well expect—the edges are apt to be uneven, bruised and marked from the drawer being opened and shut, sometimes not so gently (see illustration 146). The primary surface is also likely to show occasional scratches and blemishes from use. Small indentations and scratches will be especially noticeable under the keyholes of slant-top desks, the upper doors of secretary-bookcases and drawers, due to other keys on the bunch knocking against the surface below as former owners worked the locks. Note the wear marks caused by the photographed 17th century pull dropping and swinging into place after use.

The underside of the drawer, especially the runners, is an area of great wear in a case piece. Each time the drawer is opened and closed, the runners and their tracks are utilized; in even a short time signs of use and some wear will be obvious. On an 18th

145. Massachusetts, Plymouth-area oak "carver" chair, circa 1665–1680, with worn ball turned hand rest and wear on the turned arm.

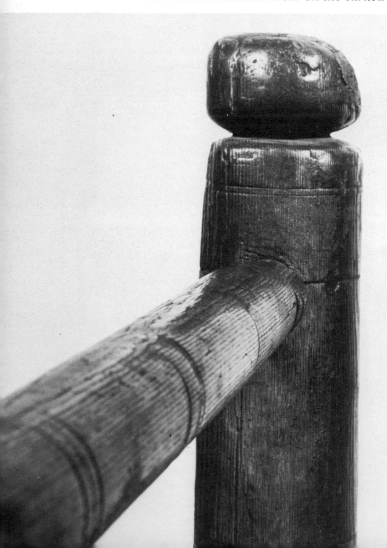

146. *Old mahogany drawer front. Note the dents and bruises on the cock-bead molding.*

147. *Signs of wear on oak drawer front, Boston chest of drawers, circa 1690–1710.*

century chest of drawers for example, evidence of wear should be extreme, even allowing for the cabinetmaker's precautionary use of reinforced hardwoods for the runners and their tracks. With careful investigation of all the drawers in a desk, one might discover that some of the runners or their tracks have been replaced. (Even the replacements may show signs of wear.) See and compare illustrations 179 and 180 on page 142 with this in mind. Although these replacements may detract from the 100% originality of the piece, the fact that they have been necessary certainly indicates wear and use over time.

148. *17th century English Carolean chair crest rail. The cupid is quite flattened with wear, as is the flower under the crown.*

149. *Clarification of carving wear on chair crest rail.*

CARVING

Carving is a very important point of wear. All carving on a piece should be examined carefully. The bits of carving that project farthest may be slightly rounded, smoothed and damaged from contact and exposure. A case in point is the carving on the back of a Carolean chair which has been rubbed smooth over the years because people have sat back against it. Other projecting areas of carving, always the most vulnerable, may well have been nicked or broken off. (Rococo Chippendale looking glasses and picture frames are such examples.) Despite the natural mishaps suffered by carved areas over time, those areas of shallow carving and thus of lower relief may remain very crisp, clear and intact. This is because the higher relief carving has served as protection (see illustration 149).

CHAPTER

12

SHRINKAGE

SHRINKAGE

The important term shrinkage is here defined as the natural reduction of the moisture content causing contraction in a piece of wood found in its final form—as a part of a piece of furniture. Wood is constantly expanding and contracting slightly as its moisture content reacts to an increase or decrease of moisture in the atmosphere. When a tree is felled in the forest, it contains more moisture than it ever will again—sometimes over 50%. (Because of this moisture, it will also weigh its greatest amount.) It is thus necessary that some drying ("seasoning") take place before a newly-cut log is worked any further, thereby naturally reducing and stabilizing the moisture content to some degree. The traditional method, air drying, was to stack the "green" logs on racks outdoors under a shelter and let the air run its natural course of evaporation over a year or two of time. The kiln-dry wood method is more often used today because it accomplishes the task very quickly—the green newly-cut wood is placed in a kiln and "seasoned" via slow heat.

Seasoned wood, with its relatively stabilized moisture content, its consequential increased stability and strength in use, and its greater resistance to decay, still reacts to some extent to changes in the atmospheric humid-

ity. Finished wood, despite this extra protection, is also subject to gradual movement.

Because shrinkage or contraction is a natural and inevitable action of all wood, old furniture made of wood will more likely than not display some signs of shrinkage. Such signs include protruding pegs, loose panels in Wainscot chairs, loose creaking joints due to tenon shrinkage and spaces between cabinet doors. It should be kept in mind that signs of shrinkage are rare with falsified pieces owing to their cores having been made from old material which has already shrunk before being used the second time.

The cyclical nature of shrinkage is demonstrated by the expansion and contraction that occurs yearly on the English late 17th century solid oak clock case door pictured here. In the first of these photographs taken during a Boston warm humid summer, the door measures its intended width—it covers the opening and the parts of the lock catch and work properly. However, in mid-January, with dry central heating conquering the 10 degree (Fahrenheit) Boston winter, great shrinkage takes place: the door has so shrunk across the grain (its width) as to cause a space between the door and the case framing and sometimes the lock is sufficiently displaced so that it no longer catches. The degree of shrinkage involved here has been dramatized in illustration 152 by placing a light in the interior of the case while the photograph was being taken.

As noted earlier, wood grain runs up and down the log (review the log drawings, illustration 10, page 20). When a log is cut into boards for use in furniture construction, the grain of each board and its direction can be determined. Even as a finished piece of furniture, the grain direction can be easily identified (see, for example, illustration 150). Once this identification has been made, it is possible to determine how wood will move according to the principle of wood shrinkage: *all wood shrinks across the grain*. Hence a

150. *The panel of an 18th century secretary door. Note how shrinkage has exposed some of its chamfered edge, meant to fit into the frame grooving. Lower on the panel it has cracked as the shrinking power has pulled the panel free from its frame which must have been holding it securely.*

151. *17th century oak clock case door with normal intended width.*

152. *17th century oak clock case door after shrinkage.*

153. *Shrinkage movement is always across the grain.*

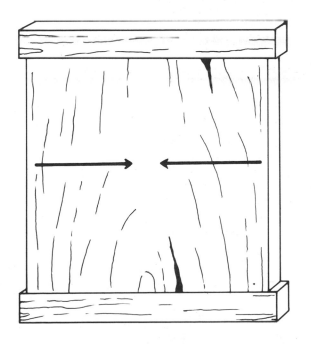

board, with time, will shrink both in width and thickness (across the grain) but not in length, which is in the direction of the grain.* This double aspect of shrinkage is called

* Contraction is much greater with plain-sawed boards (i.e., sawed tangentially to the growth rings) than those which have been radially cut (see illustration 21, page 24). (Quarter-sawed timber is obtained from a log which has been cut into four horizontal sections or quarters; each section is then radially sawed into boards or veneer although some cuts will vary from a true radial path.) Contraction also occurs more readily in lateral directions than along the axis of growth where shrinking is minute. This is because the sapwood of a tree has a higher moisture content than the heartwood, and when timber is sawn into planks, the distribution of moisture in the planks varies accordingly.

differential shrinkage. In considering the nature of shrinkage, it may be helpful to think of the common sponge—as the water dries, the sponge shrinks.

EXAMPLES OF SHRINKAGE MOVEMENT

So-called "bread-board" ends to tables and the fall fronts to slant-top desks will always show signs of shrinkage, however slight. Illustration 154 is a close-up detail of a corner of the fall front on an 18th century Boston-area mahogany slant-top desk. Because the grain of the ends (bread-boards) of the fall-front are perpendicular to the main horizontal

154. Example of bread-board shrinkage.

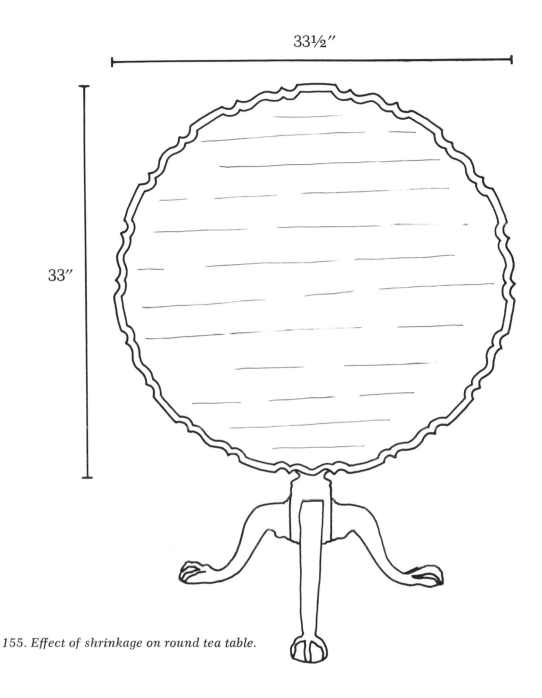

33½″

33″

155. Effect of shrinkage on round tea table.

board, whose grain runs horizontally, the large horizontal board has shrunk, as can be seen by examining the join of the horizontal and vertical boards.

Wood shrinkage is also evident upon close examination of a "round" pie-crust mahogany tea table. Upon measurement of perpendicular diameters on the table top, it will be realized that, in fact, the table is oval. This is so because the wood has shrunk across the grain and, consequently, the table is longer in the direction in which the grain runs.

Round turned legs, whether one of the heavy oak legs of a late 17th century table

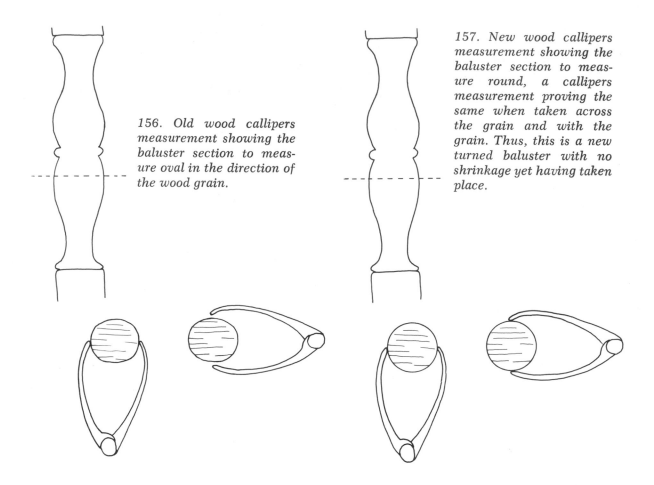

156. *Old wood callipers measurement showing the baluster section to measure oval in the direction of the wood grain.*

157. *New wood callipers measurement showing the baluster section to measure round, a callipers measurement proving the same when taken across the grain and with the grain. Thus, this is a new turned baluster with no shrinkage yet having taken place.*

or a smooth, simple, turned late 18th century Sheraton-style leg, speak to the same principle. Because wood shrinks across the grain and the wood grain runs vertically with the legs, any and all old legs will thus measure oval when measured with a callipers in two directions. Illustration 156 and 157 show how the callipers is used to prove this inevitable truth.

Shrinkage is also the cause of cracks in the sides of case pieces. The crack(s) shown in the highboy pictured here are in the direction of the wood grain (generally vertical for the sides of case pieces) and once again wood shrinkage across the grain has caused cracking. All edges of this single-board side are being held firmly to the frame of the highboy, thus the weakest area is its middle. Thus as natural shrinkage takes place, the board

gives way at the weakest point causing the crack. (As we have seen, the same principle applies to the tea table top, illustration 77, page 57.)

If more than one board were used on the side of a highboy or table top, the individual boards would often shrink across the grain and eventually pull apart, leaving spaces between them. Illustration 93, page 73, shows the top and back of an English mid-Georgian chest of drawers where several boards have been simply and crudely nailed to the carcase frame. These boards have split and spaced with shrinkage and the cabinetmaker has subsequently covered the spaces with tape—a common practice.

Shrinkage is often seen in the bottom of drawers. As several boards have been used, natural shrinkage has resulted in spaces be-

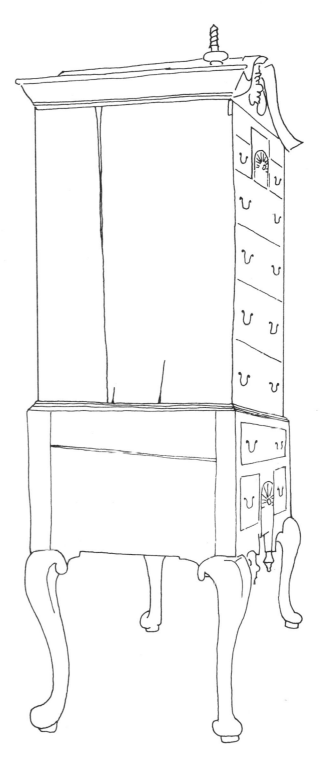

158. *18th century high chest of drawers with shrinkage crack typical of case pieces.*

tween these boards today; i.e., each board has shrunken across the grain and hence reduced slightly in width, thereby creating empty spaces. (Review drawer drawings, illustrations 64–68, pages 50–51.)

Again, we identify shrinkage movement and its exploitation in an analysis of cornerblocks. Because the wood grain of the corner-block runs in a direction contrary to the wood grain of the member it supports (see illustration 42, page 38), its shrinkage movement counter-balances the shrinkage movement of the member and thus serves its function of support to the member. This movement will, in time, cause the glue holding the block to give way (sometimes cornerblocks are also

159. Mahogany and satinwood veneered wine cooler or cellaret, circa 1795, attributed to cabinetmaker John Seymour of Boston. Note loose banding due to shrinkage.

nailed or screwed into position), although the block may remain held at one end almost indefinitely provided it does not get a knock to sever the small remaining glue area. (Photographed cornerblocks can be seen in illustrations 206 and 207, page 167.) Incidentally, due to the reduced size of the cornerblock caused by shrinkage many come loose, fall out and get lost. Therefore, one is likely to find cornerblocks missing on the underside of a chair, etc., or later inconsistent replacements.

Illustration 159 shows a handsome oval-shaped late 18th century Massachusetts wine cooler with the usual lead lining. Alternating panels of dark and light wood have been veneered onto the core wood and further decoration and support is provided by wide brass bandings. As one looks down on this cooler today, some 170 years later, one discovers large spaces between the banding and the veneer surface. Shrinkage has reduced the entire size of the piece. (Notice how it is also possible to sight down the reeded leg.)

The "spread-eagled," so-called Pembroke-style, drop-leaf table shown illustrates the unfortunate results of shrinkage. "Spread-eagling" refers to the small leaves of these tables which can no longer hang straight down thereby suggesting the spread wings of an eagle. Since these table leaves are made in keeping with the wood grain direction of their tops, when they shrink (across the grain), the leaves are drawn in until they touch the underframe when they are down, and eventually they will no longer hang properly. This is because the leaves and top have become smaller than the frame on which they rest due to shrinkage. Thus, this larger frame pushes the shrunken leaves upward. In extreme cases, the tension is finally released by the top splitting in half.

Another example of natural wood shrinkage is found in the mitre-jointed corners of picture frames or the door moldings in an old house. For seemingly no apparent reason the parts have pulled apart, leaving a gap. In fact, the wood has shrunk across the grain, thereby creating a space between the two sections (see illustrations 161 and 162).

Cracking of veneer or panels of ward-

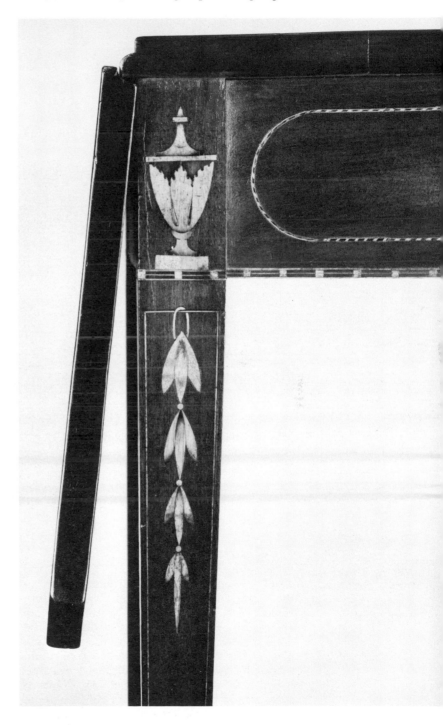

160. Detail of Baltimore mahogany drop-leaf table, 1795–1810, showing "spread-eagling."

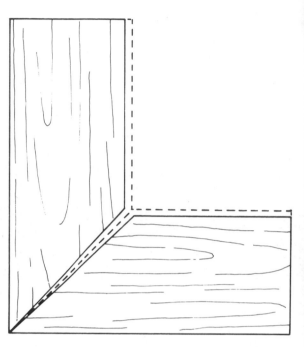

161. *Mitre-joined corner pulled apart by cross-grain shrinkage.*

162. *Japanned looking glass with mitre corner shrinkage.*

robes, sides of bookcases and cabinets, and tops of drop-leaf tables, particularly during the early 18th century when much walnut veneer was used and again during the late 18th century with the use of satinwood and other exotic veneer, is the result of shrinkage. These surface cracks in the veneer are caused by the shrinking of the core wood onto which the veneers are glued. As the core shrinks, such movement being inevitable, the top surface reacts by cracking (or moving,

too). To further complicate matters, the direction of the core wood grain was usually perpendicular to that of the veneered surface. Thus, as the core shrinkage took place, the veneer sometimes buckled. A typical example is the late 18th century mahogany veneered tall clock by Jno Kent of Manchester, England, detail shown here. Illustration 163 shows how the different directions of the two woods moving with natural shrinkage in time will cause the weaker, the veneer, to give way with cracks and buckles—or worse. The veneers themselves are unlikely to shrink to any proportionate degree because they have been cut so thin (about 1/16 of an inch on 18th century furniture) as to have inadequate power. When inlay stringing as part of the veneer surface is also involved (as in this clock case, for example), it will also react to core movement by buckling and looping up with its excess, as in illustration 187, page 148. (In general, the edges of 18th century

inlay stringing can be felt because the veneers either side have shrunk slightly away from the stringing.)

Warping is an unpredictable and most unhappy kind of shrinkage. By definition, a warped board is as it is because of irregularities in the rate or direction of shrinkage, often caused by the uneven reception of air and heat. The tendency toward warping is always present for shrinkage is not entirely uniform throughout any specimen of wood,

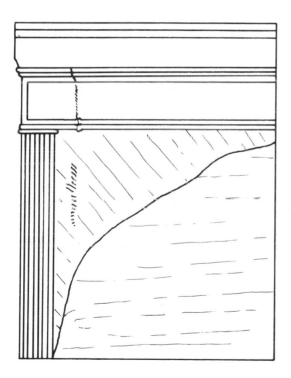

163. *Effects of natural core shrinkage movement on veneer.*

164. *18th century tall clock case with cracking, buckling, and veneer loosening problems.*

especially in woods of uneven density. Those with a straight grain and uniform texture are less prone to warping than those with interlocked, cross or spiral grains, as all these tend to shrink unevenly. Warpage (and buckling) involving this irregular wood movement beyond the normal cross-grain shrinkage usually creates havoc when it ap-

pears. It may be in the form of dishing, concave shrinkage across the grain, or in the form of twisting, spiral shrinkage. Many examples can be cited. Great character comes with the warping and shrinking of the gateleg table seen in illustrations 165 and 166.

A wonderful lesson in shrinkage is had with the study of the American mid-18th cen-

165. Warpage (and buckling) involves irregular wood movement beyond the normal cross-grain shrinkage; the top of this drawn gateleg table exaggerates such movement to better identify it.

tury Windsor chair. Here the cabinetmaker has exploited his knowledge of how and why woods shrink to produce a very sound, yet attractive chair. In addition to using a selection of woods, such as pine for the seat because it is relatively soft and easily worked for scooping to body contours, and maple or birch as legs and stretchers for their strength to withstand stress and strain, green wood was combined with seasoned wood. This green wood was used with seasoned wood so that the green pieces in drying would shrink around the dry seasoned pieces making inseparable joints and stronger chairs. Therefore, legs would be made of green wood thus shrinking (always across the grain) around

166. Warpage in the form of dishing can be recognized as part of the character of this American late 17th century gateleg table. Note the finely turned vase and ring pattern legs (turnings are deep and crisp).

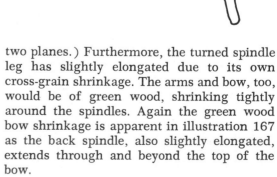

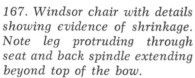

167. Windsor chair with details showing evidence of shrinkage. Note leg protruding through seat and back spindle extending beyond top of the bow.

the dry-wood stretchers. The seat would be of green wood thus shrinking around the legs and back dry wood spindles. (In fact, as in illustration 167, one sometimes sees where the legs have protruded right up through the chair seat due to the differential shrinkage of the seat; i.e., shrinkage has taken place across the grain on two surfaces—the seat top and its side—thus reducing the size on the seat on two planes.) Furthermore, the turned spindle leg has slightly elongated due to its own cross-grain shrinkage. The arms and bow, too, would be of green wood, shrinking tightly around the spindles. Again the green wood bow shrinkage is apparent in illustration 167 as the back spindle, also slightly elongated, extends through and beyond the top of the bow.

13

REPAIRS AND RESTORATION

OLD FURNITURE OFTEN shows signs of repair and restoration that have required varying degrees of skill plus considerable time, patience and ingenuity. The essence of a good repair is that it should be invisible or as nearly so as possible. Such a result can rarely be accomplished quickly or by a craftsman who does not take pride in his work.

Repairs can be classified under two headings: repairs intended to make an object strong and serviceable again (structural repairs) and repairs intended to preserve an object for posterity's eye—sometimes referred to as cosmetic repairs. Restoration can be defined as a repair which involves the insertion of a new part; like repair, it can be intended either to make a piece useable again or to return it to its proper appearance. Bear in mind, however, that 100% restoration results in a reproduction.

REASONS FOR REPAIR

It is difficult to lay down general rules as to when or where a repair or restoration is justified. This will depend on the individual case and is frequently a matter of common sense. A first consideration might be the importance of stopping further damage from taking place. A second would be the need to restore an object to its full use. When repair is decided upon, care should be taken to proceed in a way that will not mar a piece's overall appearance. Thus, if new parts are to be inserted, they will need to be given an appearance of age and wear so as to match their surround; in fact, how well this is done determines a good restoration. The new wood graft should also be consistent with the old in kind, color, grain and finish. If one chair out of a set of chairs, for example, requires a new front stretcher and all of the other chairs have worn stretchers, it would seem appropriate to make the restoration as invisible as possible by treating the new stretcher of the same wood specie and matched color with a spokeshave, chisel and sandpaper to produce the effects of wear.

When a piece of old furniture is intended for a museum or already is part of a collection (thereby implying no further use or wear), by leaving repairs in plain view confusion is avoided for the student of period detail. It must be admitted, however, that many pieces in museums have had later additions which have been "antiqued" (made to blend with their surround). They may also have had repairs and restoration which have become old and worn in themselves as a consequence of subsequent usage before they found their way into the museum. Photography is very helpful in the investigation of repairs since the sur-

168. *Replacement hinge restoring the fall front of this slant-top desk to use. The hinge is a suitably old one of wrought-iron with old screws but its size has necessitated surface patching.*

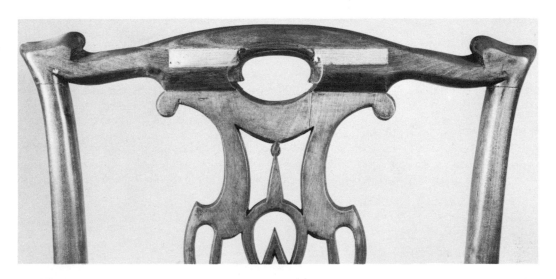

169. *"White wood" repair on an
18th century Chippendale style
carved chair back. No attempt
has been made to disguise the
new-wood insertions.*

170. *Brewster-type "great chair"
from the Massachusetts Plym-
outh area, 1640–1660, of maple
and ash. Spindles beneath the
arm include two 19th century
replacement spindles and two
inverted original spindles. The
ball hand rests on the front posts
are also replacements.*

face of a repair in a large photograph will
appear different from the surrounding wood.

There are occasions when an owner may
decide to "retire" a piece of furniture in weak
or faulty condition in order to conserve its
total originality. For example, the old rush
seat on a ladderback chair, though weak

and tattered and unsafe for use, may be retained and the chair withdrawn from use for
the sake of preserving the old rush. Broken
structural parts should always be made good,
however, and that as soon as possible after
breakage. Missing moldings should be replaced and a badly smashed corner needs

attention. A surface finish, however, should never be stripped unless it is in such bad condition that there is no alternative. To clean off the patina of years so as to rid the surface of a few scratches and markings is pure vandalism. Fortunately, the high cost of repairs and restoration influences conservation in this matter.

Whatever the defect, the necessary repair should be done as quickly as possible, because the failure of one part often throws extra strain on others so that these, in turn, begin to suffer. Thus, a chair leg which has become loose involves movement in adjoining parts —causing other joints to loosen. Broken-off parts have a habit of disappearing, and it is thus wise to refix them while they are still present. When parts are first broken, the edges are sharp and clean and they can be put back in the most unnoticeable way. When left off for any length of time, the corners of these broken pieces become rounded or otherwise changed and a really clean join becomes impossible. Then, too,

171. Good repair of back leg and veneer damage repair on this Empire style chair circa 1825.

172. Bad repair of joint, back leg with seat rail, and of damaged veneer on this American Empire style mahogany side chair.

cleaning and handling results in furniture cream or grease finding its way to the newly exposed surfaces which are to be glued; all of this has to be removed if the glue is to do its work properly.

Perhaps the biggest problem is that of replacing parts when there is no means of knowing what the originals were like. Whenever possible, the new component should be matched to an old one, otherwise the repairer will have to rely on his knowledge of period styles and his eye for balance and scale.

A repair should not lower the value of an article. Given the condition of a chair as needing repair, its value should increase if the repairs are made invisible and structurally sound. This seems straightforward but many "repairers" do not behave accordingly. They undertake a repair too difficult for them, thereby often destroying the piece, or they make repairs which are not reversible, i.e., cannot be undone, despite improved materials and greater craftsman skills in the future. Diverted saw-edge fasteners, more commonly called "corrugated dogs," for example, are sometimes useful strenghtening devices, provided they are hammered in straight and not bent over and if they are used in comparatively heavy timbers. Put in badly, or in thin or small timber sections, they are potential instruments of destruction. Using nails, likewise, despite their indispensability in woodworking, should seldom be part of the wood repairer's activity. It is often necessary to repair additional damage to already damaged woodwork caused by the misguided use or overuse of nails. Even screws, when used too near a fracture, or in too delicate or weak a part, or too long or in too heavy a gauge, can add to the destruction. The number one repairing tool for the woodworker is glue!

All complicated repair and restoration work should be placed in the hands of an experienced and knowledgeable craftsman. This is especially true for furniture of importance, in terms of age, design and tradition. The intent of this chapter is not to provide a "how to" manual for repairs. However, a few comments on the main categories of repair and restoration may be helpful to the reader as a guide to the problems inherent in old furniture which may, ultimately, require repair or restoration work.

THE REPARATION OF CHAIRS

There is probably a greater variety of problems in chair repairs than in any other piece of furniture. This is largely because of the many forms a chair takes, and because a chair is subjected to more strain and has to put up with more abuse than any other kind of furniture. In normal use it must take the weight of a person and frequently must withstand the strain of being leaned back upon by the sitter and even being tilted onto its back legs. Other stresses are applied when a chair is knocked over backwards or comes into contact with obstacles while being carried.

Faults may vary from a simple local fracture or the breakage of an arm or leg, to the loosening of some or all of the joints. When only a single joint or pair of joints has given way, it is often possible to put things right by regluing without disassembling the entire piece. An experienced cabinetmaker tries to avoid taking the whole chair apart unless all the joints are loose, since further damage could easily be caused. A general rule in fact is to always do the minimum, for in attempting the maximum repair it is easy to make things worse.

Again, because of the many stresses and demands put upon a chair, all of its parts are vulnerable. For the sake of design, many of these parts are highly impractical for their purpose—for example, the pierced and carved shield-shaped back of a Hepplewhite-style side chair. Illustration 174 pictures a Chippendale-style chair back with damage on the top rail and on some areas of the splat. The inherent weakness in this delicate back prevents it from standing up to much wear and strain, even if it is in good condition.

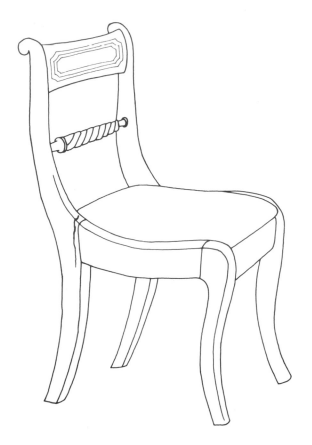

173. English Regency chair, with detail showing crack in the back stile caused by leverage placed on the chair back.

174. Damaged and partially repaired Chippendale style chair back.

THE REPARATION
OF TABLES

The chief troubles that occur with table tops are those of warping, broken joints and splits. Warped table tops have always been a problem for which there is no totally satisfactory solution. As noted in Chapter 12, warpage is especially likely to occur when the wood grain is of an unusually twisty character. Often the warpage is in the form of the top's edges curling upward—probably because wood tends to curl toward the light. As a rule, too, the face surface is polished and so sealed, whereas the lower surface is left bare, allowing moisture from the air to enter beneath and so swell the grain.

Attempts have often been made to counteract warpage by dampening the concave area and reversing the top for a few hours. This is of little use, for the table top resumes its curved shape as it dries out. The moisture will scarcely penetrate the polish, and it is likely to mark the surface instead.

When a warped table top is fixed to a rigid underframe and is not too thick, it is sometimes possible to clamp it down and screw afresh, thus holding it in a flat position. This however is done on the assumption that the false top or top rails of the understructure are firmly in position—otherwise, the curved and warped top will lift them.

When the table is of no special value, a simple though drastic cure is to cut the top into strips, plane the edges to give a flat surface, and glue up afresh. An extra piece is inserted to allow for the waste in saw dust and shavings. This, of course, cannot be done when the top is polished or of finely figured wood, since it would destroy both the polish and the figure. An alternative and almost as dramatic a cure would be to make a series of cuts along the length on the underside about ⅔ of the thickness of the wood in depth, clamp flat and glue in strips of the same kind of wood where necessary.

The above method is effective if properly done, but calls for careful consideration. If the cuts are too deep, the wood is liable to show a series of flats, this being especially marked if the cuts are wide apart. If the spacing is too wide, the local bending becomes obvious; when the cuts are closer together there is less local bending in each, since the total bend is spread over a greater number.

When joints have failed, the only plan is to "shoot" the joint anew with glue. If care is taken, it is possible to avoid the planing of the surface afterwards, always an important advantage when the table top is polished.

Splits along the grain of the wood, as distinct from failed joints, require an entirely different treatment. It is useless to rub in glue and clamp together unless the split is

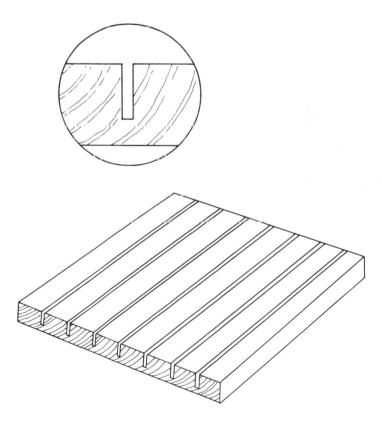

175. *Grooving for the correction of a warped table top.*

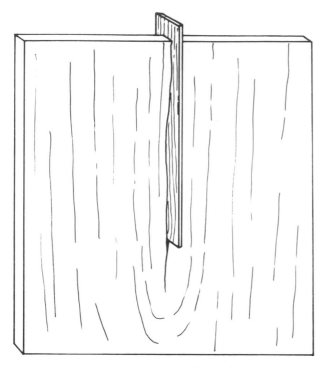

176. Reparation of split with wood insert

very slight—it will invariably open again because the wood is under considerable stress. One satisfactory solution is to open the split slightly, clean out any old polish or wax and lay in a strip of wood which matches the grain of the old as closely as possible. Another successful treatment is a supporting wood inset, butterfly-shaped to hold the two sides of the split together. This is called a dovetail key. An example of this is seen on the underside of the Chippendale-style tip-top tea table shown here.

THE REPARATION OF CASE PIECES

Case furniture—since it involves mechanical moving parts (especially drawers)—inevitably shows signs of usage and thus need of repair. Friction takes its toll, and the strain of a drawer constantly being pulled open involves considerable wear, particu-

177. Dovetail key repair

larly when the drawer is laden beyond its capacity (and most drawers usually are). However, no one expects or wishes drawers to have sharp edges and perfect fitting after 100 years or more of active service. (An example of wear on the drawer of a secretary-bookcase is seen in illustration 146, page 117.)

Problems typical of drawers include broken or loose joints, worn sides, broken and shrunken drawer bottoms and worn runners. When the corner joints of a drawer are loose, there is only one thing for the cabinet-maker to do—separate and reglue the parts. Worn drawer runners are always a problem. When it is possible to remove and replace them (or remove and reverse them), this is often an advantage, though it is still necessary to make good the wear across the front rail. Sometimes it is impossible, or awkward, to remove the runners, or there may be a solid piece from front to back rather like a shelf, and it becomes necessary to make good the deeply worn troughs.

Another variety of repair requiring yet further skills on the part of the cabinet-maker is that involved with the lathe. Candlesticks, turned legs and turned spindles all spun on the lathe, may require total replacements. In the case of the typical old Windsor chair turned leg, now oval from cross-grain shrinkage with time, the new part, after turning, must be carved down to oval measurement, to match the original. A break in a chair spindle may sometimes involve grafting, replacing a section of the spindle with the new wood. The necessary amount and size will dictate the required new turning; when ready, the new section can be whittled to the old or dowelled together. Hide glue should always be used on such occasions rather than white glue which, as was noted earlier, is so strong that the parts are unlikely to separate should later repairs make this necessary.

An alternative method of repair, when it is desirable to use as much of the old spindle as possible, is to run a metal rod up

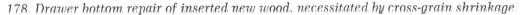

178. Drawer bottom repair of inserted new wood, necessitated by cross-grain shrinkage.

through the spindle, thus holding together and strengthening the parts. A lathe would be used to bore the hole up through the old spindle. This is a very intricate repair and requires the experience and skill of an accomplished cabinetmaker for successful results.

Fitting is an initial and important consideration in much repair work. Broken parts

179. *Worn runners. Note the troughs in the runners and veneer damage and wear on the surface rail.*

180. *Repaired runners. The troughs have been filled in and the veneer replaced. The drawer now travels on the runner smoothly.*

should be fitted together dry before the addition of glue, to determine damage, missing bits and how best to repair. Chairs and table frames should always be fitted square and then glued and clamped up dry. However, if old marks indicate the original fitting to have been made uneven and off-square, the new fitting should return parts to the original spots. Likewise, if a piece has become warped or uneven causing off-square measurements, new fittings of broken parts should not attempt to change this state of affairs.

THE REPARATION OF VENEER

Almost all furniture made from panels veneered over solid timber, unless correctly built and carefully maintained, will eventually need restoration or some form of surface repair. In addition to accidental damage, extremes in climatic conditions (especially when pieces of furniture are moved to warmer climates) and the drying effects of central heating often aggravate damage.

Veneer is particularly prone to three kinds of damage. The first of these is the superficial damage to the polished surface caused by wear and tear. This can usually be repaired by polishing procedures. The second is the damage which occurs to decorative veneers, inlays, bandings, and ornaments, often resulting from loss of adhesion at the glue line. The third kind of damage that affects veneered old furniture (this type is both the most common and the most serious) results from movement in the groundwork, which may either have swollen or shrunken, causing twisting, warping or splitting of the surface veneer. (An example of clock case movement can be seen in illustration 164, page 129.)

"FORCE AND FIX" REPARATIONS
There are several methods of dealing with warped groundworks in solid wood, depending on whether a veneered panel is to be removed first. Boards may be flattened by mechanical pressure or by changing the hu-

midity, but any attempt to return the board to its original shape by means of steaming or wetting the board will only provide a temporary remedy—the board will return to its warped condition when it dries out.

A more permanent cure can be achieved by pulling the board flat and securing it in place. This "force and fix" technique is most likely to succeed if: a) the board is not too hard, b) the board is not too thick, c) there is something substantial to secure the board to and d) if the additional supports will not spoil the appearance of the piece. The back of the board is wetted either by steam or by covering with wet sawdust and left overnight. The board is then fastened between four cross-bearers which are progressively tightened. Or, as an alternative, the back is well sized and hand-veneered, with plenty of moisture on the veneer backing, and clamped flat under pressure and allowed to dry out for a long period. When the panel is released from pressure, it is immediately fastened securely to the core.

If the panel is veneered and the original veneer is not to be removed, or the board is too thick to flatten by either of the above

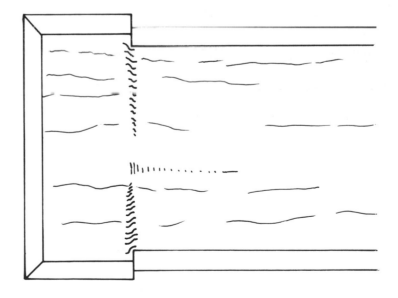

181. *Veneer buckling due to ground work reduction or shrinkage.*

methods, the board should be grooved. If the veneer has been removed, the board may be sawed into narrow strips, planed true and edge-jointed so that alternate strips have their heartwood sides opposed to equalize and distribute their different tendencies to curvature—and thus warping. (Remember, sapwood has a higher moisture content than heartwood, so that distribution of moisture in the cut board varies. The moist parts will shrink more than the drier parts causing the possibility of warpage.) It may be necessary to add a further strip to make up the original width. The whole is then planed level, resulting in a slightly thinner board.

When the board is thin, it is often possible to hand-veneer the back in strips, leaving about 4″ between strips 6″ wide. This will enable the amount of pull to be controlled. Further strips can be added as necessary. Sometimes veneer strips laid diagonally to the corners will correct a minor warp.

"DOUBLING-UP" REPARATIONS

When a board is wormy or defective in other ways, such as from insect attack or rot, it is sometimes practical to plane off the old board, down to a thickness of $\frac{3}{16}$″, and bond a new board to this remaining original. This bonding should be accomplished by gluing the heart side (the stronger side) of the new board (well seasoned and of proper kind), to the remains of the old one.

This "doubling-up" technique can also be used to cure a warped panel. Sometimes a combination of methods gives best results. Where the panel can be removed completely, slots are sawn in the back and the whole is flattened. After strips have been glued into the slots, a backing board is bonded heartside to the original.

If a new board has to be used as a completely new replacement, it should be well-seasoned, radially cut timber. If only one veneer is to be used, it is laid on the heartside with the minimum of moisture or heat. Wherever possible, an under-veneer is first laid across the grain and the face veneer, laid with the grain. For best work, both sides of the board should have under-veneers, and the backing veneer should be of the same strength and width as the face veneer and laid at the same time.

REPARATION OF EDGES
AND CORNERS

More common faults of veneer occur in corners and edges, as these are easily chipped. Areas which are handled frequently, or where moving parts create friction, such as drawer and door edges, are very prone to damage. Drawer rails often suffer in this way, particularly when the veneer is thin. (An example of such damage can be seen in illustration 139 on page 107.) However, much old furniture veneer was as much as ⅛″ thick and more in the nature of a facing. As seen in Chapter 10, in all early work the veneer was sawn by hand, and during the

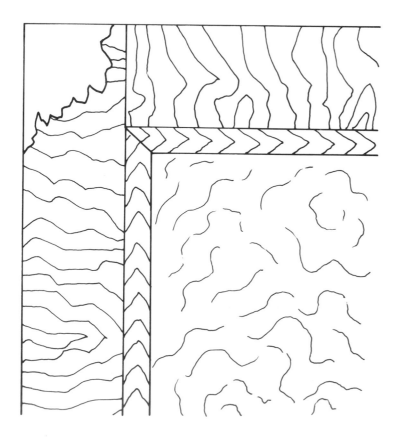

182. *Typical veneer damage to a surface corner resulting from abuse or loss of adhesion at the glue line.*

*183. Poorly matched wood repair—in grain
direction, wood type, figure and color—for
the top surface of this chest of drawers. Note
the unfortunately irregular shapes of the repair pieces.*

*184. Well matched wood repair
insert; the grain direction is the
same, the kind and figure of the
wood is similar, and the color is
quite close. The lines of the
repair are as unnoticeable as
possible.*

19th and early 20th centuries the best veneers were saw-cut by machine rather than
sliced by knife. Today, it is difficult to buy
saw-cut veneer and it is often necessary to
saw veneers by hand or on a circular saw to
enable a repair to be completed.

The treatment for a chipped corner or
edge depends largely upon the grain and
figure of the veneer. If it is of a curly, well-
marked variety, the cabinetmaker endeavors
to follow it as far as possible, selecting a
new patch which matches as closely as it can.

To make a pattern for the new veneer,
a piece of paper is held over the corner and
the heel ball is rubbed over it, thus making

the outline. The new veneer is held in a position to give the nearest match of grain, and
the paper stuck to it. The outline is cut round
with a fine fret-saw and finally trimmed to
shape by trial and error with a file. When
ready, it is glued into position and rubbed
down, with tape stuck over the joint to prevent it from opening as the glue dries out.
If it does tend to lift, a flat block can be
warmed and clamped over it with newspaper
between. (This softens the glue again so that
it will hold.) It is desirable for new veneer
to be slightly thicker than the old so that it
can be levelled later without interference to
the surrounding surface.

Veneered drawer rails frequently suffer damage, either due to the drawer itself catching the veneer or because of excessive wear at the ends. (See illustration 179.) This veneer should be relatively thick but, regardless of its thickness, it is essential that the worn wood at the back be made good and sound first. Usually straight-grain veneer is used on these rails.

BUBBLES AND BRUISES

When veneer has lifted locally in the form of a bubble, it usually implies that the glue beneath has perished. Thus it is of little use to apply a hot caul over it. What is necessary is the introduction of fresh glue. In order to accomplish this, the cabinetmaker makes a cut through the veneer following the grain direction. This cut enables the veneer at each side to be pressed down so that glue can be introduced by a slip of veneer or a thin palette knife. After gluing, it is important to clamp a warm block over the surface with newspaper interposed. It can usually be established whether or not the veneer is down properly by tapping with the fingernails—a hollow sound will be heard when the veneer is still raised.

Bruises in a veneered surface can be difficult to cope with in that any attempt to raise the bruise by steaming may result in the veneer being lifted. Unless the bruising is really bad, it may be best to leave it as it is. Otherwise, it is necessary to prick the surface right through the polish and veneer, place a damp rag over the affected area and apply a hot iron so that steam reaches the groundwork, tending to swell it. Unfortunately, apart from the danger of the veneer lifting, the surface finish may deteriorate, requiring further treatment.

THE REPARATION OF MARQUETRY

The repair of marquetry can be troublesome, particularly when entire pieces are missing. Usually, replacements must be made by the repairer himself, involving much work and challenge. Elaborate designs may be beyond the capacity of the cabinetmaker, but simple fan corner pieces, for example, can be recreated. The tapered pieces are prepared first and fitted together. They are usually shaded toward one edge, and this is done by holding each individual piece with a tweezer and dipping it into hot sand (similar to the heated sand used by the optician in adjusting eye glasses).

Sometimes marquetry panels have lifted in parts—often resulting in the disappearance of small pieces. If the missing pieces are not too large, replacements can be fitted into position, working from a traced outline of the design. In cases where the marquetry has lifted badly, however, the treatment may be difficult. The repairer can attempt to clamp a hot caul over the raised part, but usually the glue beneath has perished and fresh glue has to be worked in if possible. This is usually feasible when the bubble is at the edge, or when one of the pieces of marquetry has come adrift, the glue being worked in with a scrap of veneer.

When the bubble is a small local one, it is often possible to remove a piece of veneer either entirely or sufficiently for fresh glue to be inserted. When a large area has come adrift, the only satisfactory action is to raise the whole, clean off the old glue, and lay it afresh. In raising veneer for regluing, a spatula or similar flat knife should always be the first method the cabinetmaker tries for loosening the glue. Applied heat for this purpose may destroy the surface patina and finish.

One of the difficulties in working with lifted pieces of veneer and their replacements is the possibility of the replaced veneer getting out of position. Really large areas of lifted parquetry or marquetry are extremely difficult to deal with and may necessitate a hot caul being pressed over the entire surface to soften the glue. In order to preserve the pattern and parts, gummed tape should first be laid over the inlay or a thin piece of brown paper should be glued over it to hold the parts together. This is a very difficult operation and should be avoided if possible.

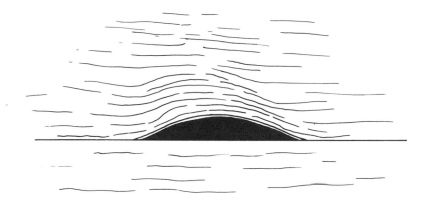

185. *Lifted veneer*

186. *Veneer bubble or blister, probably due to perished glue.*

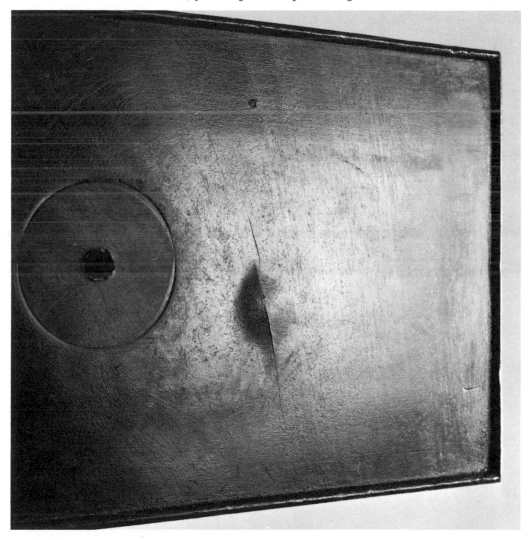

187. Early 19th century card table with decorative brass inlay stringing. Note corner where brass has lifted and looped.

Brass inlay, especially stringing, sometimes causes complications when solid groundwork shrinks across the grain. The brass is unable to accommodate itself to the reduced size and lifts, forming small loops (see illustration 187, up above). It is impossible to press down on the loop as the groove is too short or narrow for the brass. The only solution is to cut across the in-lay with a line hacksaw (or metal-cutting saw). The saw cut generally removes enough metal to enable the parts to be pressed down but, if necessary, the cut ends can be filed down a bit. The brass tends to be springy so that the repairer usually clamps a block over the inlay while the glue sets. Similar problems occur with wood inlay stringing owing to the core wood shrinkage, and similar action must be taken for correction of the difficulty.

COMBATING DAMPNESS

Occasionally a piece of furniture has been stored in a damp cellar or barn and requires attention. Typical damp-induced problems include drawers and doors which stick or bind, stiff table leaves, rusted hardware, buckled veneer, failure of glued parts in general, and a deteriorated finish.

The absorption of damp is a fairly slow process, made still slower by the finish on the piece which acts as a barrier. Movement in the wood is therefore very slow and any attempt at putting things right should be slow as well. If movement is speeded up, as it would be if the wood were brought into a hot room and left there, the glue would probably fail immediately with resulting loose joints. One should not attempt to reglue failed joints while still damp, as the glue will not hold properly.

Furniture is rarely affected by dry rot unless it has been stored in a damp unventilated cellar. Once badly attacked, however, a piece cannot be repaired as the substance of the wood itself has deteriorated. Dry rot usually belongs to the house structure, occurring there, and its treatment is drastic, involving the burning of all affected timber.

WORMHOLES

When small holes appear on the surface of old furniture, chances are that the woodworm has been at work. "Woodworm" is the term commonly applied to the species of grub or larva which germinates in wood and tunnels through, devouring and turning it to powder. Wood-boring insects generally called woodworms include the beetle families of Anobiidae, Lyctidae and Bostrichidae. Once the presence of woodworm has been detected, treatment should begin at once. Even if the surface of affected wood shows nothing more

than a few tiny holes (about $\frac{1}{16}$″ in diameter), the interior of the piece may be half eaten away. Hardwoods and softwoods, including pines, are liable to attack under proper conditions; walnut in particular suffers, whereas mahogany seems almost immune.

The beetles may have been introduced from other furniture or they may have entered through an open window, since they live in the dead branches of trees. The female lays her eggs in crevices in the wood, then dies. Small grubs hatch from the eggs and begin to burrow into the wood. They work along in this way for perhaps a year or two, leaving behind them a tunnel filled with a light, fine powder. Finally, the grub tunnels toward the surface of the wood and bores a chamber in which it lies until it turns into a chrysalis. After a few weeks it develops into a mature beetle with wings and legs, bites its way through to the wood's surface and emerges. Thus, what we call a wormhole is actually a flight hole. This ex-

188. Woodworm: the larva (or grub) stage of the furniture beetle ("worm") and the adult beetle. The most common furniture beetle or woodworm, Anobium punctatum, *is dark reddish brown in color and measures ½″ in length with parallel rows of small pits in the wing cases. The earlier stage grub or worm is cream color.*

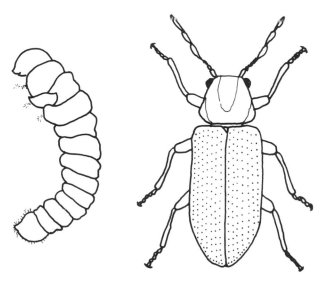

189. *Replacement pad foot on worm-ridden table leg.*

odus generally takes place during June, July and August, although it may occur as early as May. The male and female beetles mate and the entire process starts again.

The presence of holes is not proof that beetles are still at work, but it is usually possible to detect recent holes by their appearance—i.e., the edges will be sharp and the insides light yellow. Holes caused by an old colony which has died out are usually dark and half-filled with furniture wax.

The most common treatment for woodworm is the application of oil-borne organochlorine insecticides made especially for this purpose. Before application, as much powder as possible should be removed from the holes to enable the liquid to penetrate. The liquid is fed into the holes with a small brush or funnel. One treatment may not suffice since individual beetles may escape.

Another method of treatment (which does involve sending the infected furniture to a firm with the necessary equipment), is that of fumigation. The furniture is placed in a special chamber, which is then filled with a poisonous gas. This elaborate measure does not, however, prevent future attack. (A home version of fumigation, often successful, is to enclose the piece in airtight plastic with a DDT bomb and leave it there until the bomb has run its full course.)

Simple preventive measures aimed at minimizing woodworm attack and damage include keeping furniture dry (moisture content of 10% or less) and sealing the pores of large-pored woods such as oaks and ash with a finish. Action should be taken at the first signs of infection.

Where wormholes exist, the most important thing to establish is how far the structural strength of the afflicted piece has deteriorated. When the attack is only slight it is enough to treat the wood with an insecticide. If structural parts have been badly damaged, the only alternative is to replace them with sound wood, taking the precaution of rubbing the new wood with insecticide. Such affected parts as rails can sometimes be backed with sound wood, this backing being joined or screwed to whatever adjoining members there may be and glued on. This is often the procedure for veneered parts, for example, which may be unmarked on the surface but badly wormeaten in the groundwork beneath.

When a part such as a leg is so badly attacked as to be liable to snap off, and the item is required for a further period of service, there is little to be done except to replace the affected part. Sometimes it is possible to make a reasonably effective repair by cutting a groove at the back of a leg and letting in a sound strip of wood. This would enable a piece such as a side cabinet or light bureau to stand and be used, but would be of little value for a chair or table in constant service.

Repairs such as the above are relatively simple matters of replacement and fitting. It is when the "show wood" or primary wood surface is affected by woodworm that the problem becomes really serious.

PROTECTION AND CARE

Prudent care and protection should be assumed for all antique furniture. Carelessness and risk of danger should never be permitted with fine old pieces which are irreplaceable, regardless of money, skill or time. Among the simple precautions to be taken are the following. Old furniture should be kept away from strong sunlight and never left on a porch or patio. One should never stand on an old chair, especially if it has a cane or rush seat. Feet should be kept off chair rungs and trestle table bases. Desk tops made of soft pine should be covered with a blotter to avoid pen and pencil dents. And, when a loose joint is discovered or a section of veneer comes open, it should receive the immediate attention of a cabinetmaker to avoid progressive problems.

Despite normal household cleanliness, dust, dirt and grime find their way onto all flat surfaces. This, coupled with dampness, fireplace smoke, cooking vapors and cigar smoke, produces a thin film on furniture. To maintain maximum beauty, this film must be removed. A light dusting with a clean, soft cloth once or twice a week should accomplish this. About once every six months, a mild furniture wax or cream polish might be applied to surfaces in very small quantities. However, the less one puts on one's furniture, thereby minimizing build-up, the better.

As mentioned earlier, in the United States and elsewhere, where low winter temperatures demand intense central heating, a problem is created due to changes in temperature and humidity. The drying central heat reduces the humidity content which, in turn, causes the furniture to dry out, crack and shrink. Mechanical humidifiers seem one of the best counterbalancing devices for replacing the moisture content, although some wood movement is inevitable.

Dramatic wood movement often takes place when a piece of furniture of 200–300 years in age is permanently moved from one climate to another—from damp England to relatively dry Boston, for example. Little can be done to avoid or protect against such movement, and it is difficult to guess how severely a piece will be effected. In fact, it is a game of chance. When the adjustments have taken place (and this takes a year or more), a respected cabinetmaker should be consulted concerning any necessary restoration or repair.

14

FAKES

A SPURIOUS PIECE of furniture is an imitation of an old piece presented with the intention of deceiving. (The straightforward copying of old examples for sale as reproductions is legitimate commercial business and quite a different matter.) Regardless of how successful the deception may be, the collector must realize that what he is paying so dearly for is the product of modern labor and materials. The piece in question is likely to be inaccurate in historical detail and certainly does not reflect the inherent beauty and character of the past.

Many clever efforts have been made with regard to "faking" antiques. Various techniques have been employed and special pieces which were desirable at certain periods in history have been especially vulnerable to copying. Naturally, such attempts have met with varying degrees of success. The matter of faking furniture is a fascinating subject in its own right and its study provides many valuable cautionary lessons.

KINDS OF FAKE
FURNITURE

A fraudulent old piece may take several forms. This piece may be of entirely new construction—an imitation made from old wood or from wood given the signs of age artificially. Another category of fake is an imitation made up partially of genuine old furniture parts with additions or restorations carried out in new or old material. New carving and other embellishments may be executed on plain but authentic old pieces so as to enhance their value. Another form that is most successful in its deception is the piece created by the transformation of genuine old pieces or parts of them into objects of much greater value by their union with other genuine old pieces or parts of them. The result is sometimes called a "married" piece. The parts of two pieces not made together, however, will seldom "marry" without some alteration to one or both, and it is for the signs of such alterations that the collector must look. For example, are the primary and secondary woods the same throughout the piece and are the construction details of all drawers (dovetails, back joints, etc.) identical? Are the decorative details (such as crispness of carving) consistent throughout the piece? Do all the brass holes measure alike and do the brasses themselves show signs of similar age? As one approaches the Dunlap highboy pictured here, at first glance one might conclude that all was in order in terms of Dunlap style characteristics and general proportions. But closer study will reveal many inconsistencies that finally lead

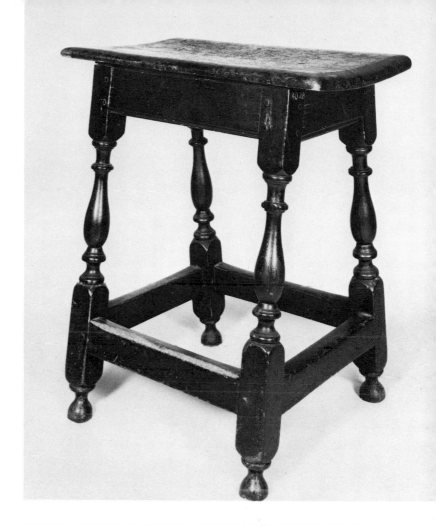

190. Early 18th century joint stool of Massachusetts maple. The use and wear of time can be seen on the worn stretchers, the warped top, and the smoothed thumb-nail molding of the top.

to the conclusion that this is a married piece. The selected detail of proof, shown in illustration 194, is a comparison of the drawer dovetails for the top and bottom parts. Obvious differences in size and craftsmanship, top and bottom, indicate that they were certainly not all made by the same furniture craftsman. (Note the variations in drawer size.)

Similar close examination should be applied to matched sets of chairs, particularly if the set is large and complete and thus very rare. Small sets of four are sometimes enlarged to eight by combining old parts with new. This can be highly deceptive when done well, and even though new parts are detected, they can be mistaken for repairs. Each chair must thus be studied carefully.

Whatever the form in which the falsified piece is found, it will be likely to approximate a rare and costly piece in great demand, for only such pieces justify by their financial return the time and effort spent by the faker —a useful thing to remember. Another general point that collectors should keep in mind is that rooms were larger in the past and thus pieces of small size and scale were rare and should be regarded with suspicion. Conversely, the likelihood of buying a large piece of furniture which is later proven spurious is relatively remote. Sideboards, for example, which seem very large by today's standards, are likely to be their original size; a small sideboard in contrast, should be inspected for signs of being cut down.

191. 20th century oak joint stool with no signs of wear or warpage: the stretchers have received little abuse, the top is straight, and the top edge thumb-nail molding is crisp.

193. Mid-18th century New ▶
Hampshire Dunlap style high
chest or highboy of maple. Photograph courtesy the Yale University Art Gallery. Mabel Brady
Garvan Collection

192. Carolean-style stool with
appropriately carved legs and
stretchers of characteristic walnut and a mellow looking patina.
Its date, however, is 1920, not
1685. Note the joint connecting
the legs and stretchers. On a period piece a mortise and tenon
joint would be used here.

THE FAKING OF DETAIL WORK

The more wonderful and rare the piece, the more it requires careful scrutiny by the collector to establish its validity. He should begin by questioning the very details which make the piece so outstanding. If the pie-crust molding on a tip-top table, for instance, checks out as always having been a part of the table and not a newly applied addition, the rest of the table can be examined with the age tests and a conclusion of authenticity reached for the table as a whole. A plain early tip-top table would be of interest and value, but a similar example with the piecrust molding intact is of even greater importance, and hence a detail of interest to the deceiver.

The wide difference in value between carved and uncarved pieces provides great incentive for the imitator to attempt to enhance the value of a piece with new carving. Flat arabesque and fret carving are often resorted to for this type of deception as they have the important advantage of allowing the face of the new ornament to retain its original surface; only the sides of the design and the background will be freshly cut. The newly cut surfaces will then be stained, waxed, rubbed and dirtied to give them the appearance of age. However, careful scrutiny should still reveal the new incisions, thus offering good proof of new work. Early chests, Bible boxes, the frieze of an oak refectory table, and the carving on Chinese Chippendale-style chairs all lend themselves to this type of carved addition.

Another opportunity for "carving up" presents itself with the knees of cabriole legs on Queen Anne and early Georgian chairs. Many knees on such chairs are known to have been carved and this carved detail, of course, adds to the value and interest of the chairs. When such carving was intended as part of the cabinetmaker's original design, he took care to leave adequate extra stock at the knee as he carved out the leg; hence the

194. Drawers of Dunlap style-high chest. Note differences in dovetailing, drawer depth and thickness of drawer fronts as well as reshaping of drawer moldings of top section to match with those of the bottom.

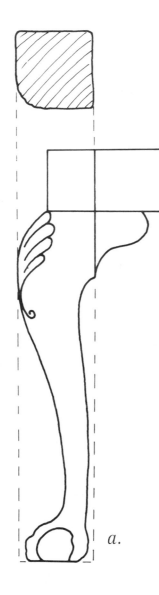

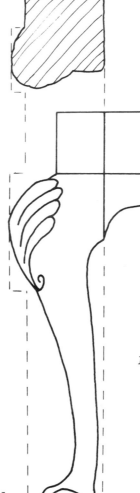

195. a. Inadequately carved knee of little projection and shallow carved detail.
b. Richly carved knee of properly proportioned contours.

baroque convex shell design shown in illustration 195 (leg *b*) has properly proportioned contours. The knee which has been carved out later (leg *a*) can quickly be detected because there will be little variety in the relief of the carving, since stock was not left for this purpose. The shallow carving looks inadequate at best and, to achieve even this, the leg has had to be carved down, possibly distorting the lines of the chair.

Another way the imitator will attempt to simulate age is by giving his carving a worn and rounded look all over. In studying genuine carving, however, it will be observed that although many prominent areas of the carving are rounded (from wear and handling) or even missing (again from wear and handling), the less prominent areas will remain as crisp and sharp as when originally carved. In fact, the mint-condition pieces (and hence the most desirable) have aged gracefully with their edges retained and carving intact.

Fake new inlay work on the appropriate styles of furniture (such as late 18th century

Hepplewhite and Sheraton pieces, etc.) also serves to enhance the appearance and value of a piece of furniture, and thus becomes another skill for the imitator to master. New wood inlays can be laid in newly cut beds in the surface of the old satinwood veneer surface, for example, and then scraped down to the general surface level. As the new glue dries, it will contract, thus the newly inlaid wood will, at times, sink below the rest of the surface. When this happens, the new inlay bed cuts are exposed and the foul play becomes obvious. A characteristic of old inlay stringing and other decorative details is the difference in surface when compared with the surrounding areas. Usually the inlays will feel higher, a subtlety caused by wood movement over time, and almost impossible to create anew.

Yet another detail, which increases the interest and thus the value of a piece, is the addition of corner brackets to a table or chair which has been without them. To add fretwork brackets to an otherwise very simple card table, for example, will increase its beauty and interest—assuming this is done carefully and in keeping with the table. Since there are many varieties of decorative bracket which can be used in several different places, constant alertness is necessary.

THE FAKING OF REPLACEMENT PARTS

Another and major fakery effort involves the introduction of new materials into pieces of furniture to replace missing or worn-out parts. This work is often essential in order to preserve a piece and to permit it to carry on its original purpose. All new materials should of course match the old in terms of exact kind, age, and color. However, because such restoration work is not always identified but rather concealed with the intention of the piece maintaining its "100% originality," value and interest, the collector and buyer must be on constant guard.

A case in point might be the necessary replacement of a 17th century oak refectory table top. To locate wide oak boards of the proper age and character with appropriate signs of wear and patina would be impossible were it not for the availability of old oak floorboards and ship deck timbers. Of course such boards have nail holes at fairly regular intervals, and these would have to be filled in or disguised in some way. An example of the problems involved in this kind of work can be seen by examining the simple American trestle table pictured in illustration 196. At first glance it appears consistently old and appropriate for its 130 year age. Closer scrutiny reveals unexplained and unlikely markings on the boards plus unreasonable, evenly spaced, filled nail holes along the edges of the boards. The history of this table is known; the table top was created in the early 20th century from fine barn floorboards which had been nailed down. Further markings are explained by the wheels of a wheel barrel marring the surface.

The tripod table with its circular top is a most desirable piece of furniture in today's market, and hence forgeries are common. Discarded pole screens or damaged torcheres are cut down and circular tops are added. These tops sometimes come from damaged dumbwaiters, but more frequently are newly turned from old mahogany. Measuring the table top for shrinkage will usually show up new turning, since, as we have seen, wood shrinks across the grain and an old top will therefore be slightly oval. (To achieve this proper ovoid shape, a faker will sometimes bake the new round part, thereby causing artificial shrinkage, cracking and checking.) Careful attention should also be given to the way the base and top are joined together. Clues indicating that the two pieces have recently been joined include disturbed wood surface, new finish and modern construction methods.

Another example of careful and skillful deception is the necessary replacement of legs on a case piece, such as a highboy or a high chest. By sawing off the original legs just below where they join the vertical corner blocks or the apron, minimum disturbance of the piece takes place. Substitute legs are

196. *Trestle pine board table made from barn floor boards. The boards individually measure widths of 14", 13" and 15". Note the marks from the spiked wheel of a wheel barrow.*

then dowelled in the base of the corner posts and the inner parts of this new joint are stained to aid in its disguise.

Yet another opportunity for successful deception presents itself in the form of the unusually high office desk, about 38″ high from floor to writing surface, often pictured in the stories of Charles Dickens. High stools were used with these desks. With little difficulty the feet can be removed from these desks, the bottom drawer eliminated, and the projecting sides cut into feet, thereby reducing the desk to the standard and more acceptable height.

Recently, a mahogany chest of drawers came under special scrutiny due to several ink stains and unusual scratches apparent on the side wood surfaces. Further investigation revealed that this wood had once been part of a Victorian table top. Such signs of former and alien use are indeed helpful in judging the 100% originality of a piece. Careful study of the fine mid-18th century American dressing table or lowboy shown here reveals that the top is a replacement. In spite of the careful craftsmanship involved, including an appropriate edge molding, even in a photograph the wood looks different—too smooth without signs of wear, a suggestion of different color, and no patina or feeling of age.

Another example of table top alteration

197. Close-up of the trestle table showing one of a series of suspicious nail holes.

198. Mid-18th century mahogany dressing table with a replacement top that lacks signs of age or use.

199. Early 18th century gateleg table with later top and drop-leaves.

and replacement is seen in illustration 199. Early 18th century gateleg tables such as this can be found with these proportions but invariably the top and hanging leaves are each made of one piece of wood—not of several pieces as here represented. Therefore, the conclusion must be that the top is a later replacement (assuming the base is old).

THE FAKING OF WORMHOLES

Fake wormholes have traditionally been associated with the falsifying of antique furniture. The dramatic means of achieving a wormhole effect have ranged from shotgun holes to acid and drills. It is actually quite easy to create wormholes; it is also quite easy to prove their authenticity. A soft copper wire when inserted into a wormhole will enter straight and extend deep into the hole if the wormhole is, in fact, the product of a drill. If the wire follows a meandering path it is likely that a "worm" has been there (see Chapter 13). Signs of sawdust near the entrance to the hole offer further evidence of a wormhole's authenticity; worm which is still active can be detected by tapping the wood sharply when a fine sawdust should fall from the holes.

Because wormholes are considered such a time-worn indication of antiquity, it is all the more important to be on guard against attempted fakery. Quite often one is presented with wood showing the meandering tunnels on the wood's surface as final proof that the piece is very old. But it should be remembered that the "worm" travels his devious route within the wood, only coming to the surface to depart and creating a "hole" with his exit. (These "flight holes" are never all precisely the same shape and size and are seldom exactly at right angles to the wood surface.) Sometimes exposed worm tunnels are legitimate due to extreme wearing away of the wood, such as on the arms of an early chair, but this is not generally the case. More typical is a 17th century oak chest recently brought to my attention whose back and bottom were constructed of old tunnelled wormy wood. In order to use this very old wood for replacement parts in this chest, the wood had to be cut, and thus the worm tunnels became exposed. "Worms" simply do not travel along the surface, so this wood could not be original to the chest. One therefore can well speculate on the original shape of the worm-riddled table leg pictured in illustration 190.

When an imitator while working a piece of old wood happens to cut through a worm tunnel longitudinally, rather than sectionally, and the long tunnel appears on the surface, he may fill it in with wax or another filler for concealment. This kind of deception is never permanently successful—the filling eventually sinks or falls out, revealing the tunnel.

An ironic fact is that the informed collector prefers genuine furniture without wormholes as a sign of supposed age. (Genuine wormholes need not be old.) He realizes that a piece affected by worms is being slowly depreciated in both strength and value. He also realizes that eradication of the worm is extremely difficult and that the radical treat-

200. *Woodworm channels legitimately exposed on the surface of this late 17th century chair hand rest where the wood has been worn and smoothed away by use.*

ment involved will probably destroy the patina, further depreciating the value and beauty of the piece.

THE FAKING OF SURFACES

With lacquered and painted furniture, an antique appearance is sometimes achieved by emphasizing the cracks. These fraudulent pieces are usually made of pine. Once the surface is rubbed down, several coats of special paint are applied, the last coat being the color of the ground. The design is then drawn on and the raised portions applied. When the design has been gilded, the surface is treated with a thin coat of French polish, then topped with a coating of stiff paste or starch. The strong drawing power of the paste causes the surface of the polish to crack. The paste is then washed away and a dark colored wax is worked into the artificial cracks thereby emphasizing them. Cracks made in this manner will be large and wide, similar in character to the cracks found in old oil paintings. They can easily be distinguished from the cracks seen on genuine lacquer or gilding which are very fine. An example of an old gilded looking-glass with hair line cracks is shown in illustration 132, page 101.

The color of the interior surfaces of genuine old lacquered pieces such as the insides of cabinet doors will be brighter than outside surfaces because they are less exposed to the effects of light and atmosphere. The color of the lacquer underneath the escutcheon plate covering the keyhole has also been protected from light and should thus appear brighter if the lacquer finish is indeed old.

On a genuine piece of gilt furniture, such as a table, it will be noticed that the portions of the table that face upwards will be dark in comparison with those parts which face downwards. This is due to dust having collected on the upturned part and slowly darkened the surface of the gilding. This sullying effect of dust can be recognized on an old gilt picture frame; if the frame has always been hung in the same position, the bottom upturned side will be perceptibly darker than the inside top of the frame which faces downward. This darkening effect of dust, although more accentuated on original gilt pieces of the early 18th century, is also discernible on pieces gilded as recently as 25 or 30 years ago. This observation, therefore, can only be used as a test for gilding of quite recent manufacture. The faker does not often imitate this undoubted but subtle sign of a certain age.

Another relatively sure way to identify the faked imitation of old gilding is if the gilding has been applied onto a red ground. This is particularly noticeable because the imitator, in order to simulate the appearance of age, rubs off the gilding, exposing the ground beneath. Gold does not tarnish but it does mellow with accumulated dust and dirt. To tone down the brightness of recently applied gold, the imitator uses a wash of stain over the gilt surface. For detection, this surface can be gently wiped, thus removing the stain and exposing the bright gilding beneath. It will take two or three years for the surface to become sufficiently hard to resist this test.

The accessories of a piece of fake furniture also require "work." Stories of burying brasses in the ground to achieve an old look and dipping them in acids and abrading them with flails to create the impression of wear contain much truth. Many methods were, and still are, tried and used—the desired final result being for brasses and hinges to appear worn, old and original to the piece. Old nails can be fabricated in the old hand-forged way and then "aged" by some of the above suggested methods. Alternatively, Victorian cut-nails can simply be hammered, thereby simulating the handwork of the earlier nails. The best defense against fake accessories is to seize all opportunities for studying genuine hardware.

CAUTIONS
FOR COLLECTORS

Fascinating deeds of fakery can be discussed ad infinitum, but the main purpose here is to instill caution. Late period sideboards, for example, become more desirable (and hence profitable) when today's imitator cuts off the round legs and fixes tapered square legs onto the stumps. In purchasing a sideboard, therefore, the collector should always examine the legs where they join the core stock to ensure that this substitution has not been carried out. Another current trick is to take the heavy legs of an Empire style dining room table and turn them down on a lathe into legs of earlier styles, thereby enhancing the beauty and current value of the table.

The shrewd collector should always pay special heed to the tops of tall clocks, the tops of highboys, and other remote areas to which the imitator is likely to have paid the least attention. Nothing helps the collector more than examining furniture in natural daylight. In artificial light it is very difficult to perceive gradations of color which in daylight can easily be observed. The variation in wood color between old and new parts and the differences in their surface condition are more easily discerned in full daylight, and the efforts of the imitator to hide restored parts by staining the wood will also become ap-

201. Top of highboy. A good place to look for signs of deception.

202. *Knee-hole mahogany desk, 1765–1775, made by Edmund Townsend (1736–1811). A fine example of Newport design and craftsmanship, this desk is uniquely documented with an original label on the upper side of the top drawer bottom (see detail, illustration 203).*

parent in natural light. It should be remembered that new wood tends to fade more than the older wood surrounding it; thus, a new wood replacement or repair will appear lighter unless it initially has been stained darker to compensate for this greater fading. Questionable stained and dirtied wax can be scratched or removed with a fingernail (or even rubbed off a furniture surface) and its presence is a sure sign of a faked surface.

Careful inspection of drawers is another way to guard against fakes. The interiors of early drawers and cabinets are surprisingly clean and fresh looking. It is impossible for the imitator to reproduce this appearance. Attempts are made to do so, however, by staining with analine dyes, painting the interiors in oil colors (usually green or brown) or "wallpapering" the drawers with old newspapers or blue paper, this having been the fashion at one time. Another attempt is the practice of spilling ink inside the drawers, particularly those of a chest of drawers or a desk.

The wise collector will always exercise caution when presented with a pedigree (history) for a piece of furniture. All pieces of antique furniture must have pedigrees but these should be carefully validated. The antique dealer's familiar quote, "Oh, I bought this chair from a wonderful little old lady who inherited it from her grandmother," may indeed be appealing and sell chairs, but it must be recognized for what it is—a clever sales pitch.

Unscrupulous antique dealers have been known to show great dishonesty concerning pedigrees. Fine pieces are sometimes "planted" in a country house implying that they have been in the family's possession for a number of years. Or it will be falsely claimed that a piece from a certain collection was purchased at a given auction. Many times these facts can be checked if the effort is made.

Dealers and collectors alike are impressed with cabinetmakers' labels found on old pieces of furniture. Such labels make a piece of furniture much more interesting in that some of its history can be learned. And if a certain cabinetmaker's work is especially

fine and desirable, the piece becomes most valuable as the identified product of his work. Here shown is the only known labeled piece of furniture made by Edmund Townsend of Newport. Needless to say, however, a label may not be genuine and thus should be held in suspicion at all times. Labels can be very simple things to reproduce given the knowledge of old techniques and the proper old tools, and imitators have become most successful in this regard.

A favorite practice of faking labels is to clip a cabinetmaker's advertisement from an old newspaper or city directory and paste it

203. Detail, Edmund Townsend label. Photograph courtesy the Museum of Fine Arts, Boston.

to a piece of old furniture. The letterhead of an old bill will serve the same purpose. This type of faking can be recognized by the lack of decorative borders and the difference in typography. Labels made from newspaper advertisements have distinctively small type. Moreover, if such a "label" is moistened and removed, the printing on the back will serve as a give-away—genuine labels were never printed on the back. Thrilling as it would be to discover an original label on a piece of old

furniture, one would be foolish to place great store by such a discovery. (For more about labels see Chapter 15.)

Unless the maker of spurious furniture

205. *Ear piece or knee bracket of Philadelphia Chippendale-style chair of questionable age: the carving is smooth, careful and "clean" on the secondary surfaces without the characteristic exuberant and impatient signs of hand craftsmanship. The C-scroll carved edge moldings on the front seat rails are applied; period counterpart moldings are carved from the solid wood as in illustration 204.*

204. *Ear piece or knee bracket of Philadelphia 18th century chair; hand-tooling marks are clearly visible and can be easily felt on the secondary wood surfaces.*

206. *Old cornerblock 18th century Philadelphia Chippendale-style chair. Hand-planing marks can be seen on the cornerblock and on the inside seat rail. The smoky look of time is present (recall our discussion of patina) and signs of wear can be found on the chair stile and seat rail edge.*

207. *New stained pine cornerblock, Philadelphia Chippendale-style chair. Hand-planing marks can be found. An attempt has been made to suggest an aged "patina" on the interior surface including "dirt" placed in the corners of the cornerblock. There are no signs of wear. The Benjamin Randolph label is genuine, however.*

limits himself to trying to produce an exact replica of a good old piece, he will invariably commit an error in the proportion or ornamentation of his ware. Torn between the desire to produce a passable antique and the desire to increase its selling potential, he may make a piece's dimensions smaller to better suit today's smaller rooms, or he may be tempted to produce a "unique" or "rare" piece of furniture. Errors of dimension and proportion may be coupled with misuse of decoration on pieces of a given style. By careful study of genuine pieces, the collector can become familiar with the general characteristics peculiar to each period. (A case in point would be the seat of a mid-18th century mahogany side chair whose seat always appears —and should appear—too big when one looks straight down on it.)

It must be pointed out that the subtleties of old furniture can be reproduced by a man who knows his business as a faker —a skillful cabinetmaker using genuine pieces as models and wood of the proper kind and age. There have been some famous practitioners, known by name, of this type of deceit who have known as much about old furniture as the museum people and other professionals who finally judged their creations. Such situations lead to fascinating battles of wits between experts. In the case of a really good faked piece of furniture, the novice has no chance whatsoever of making a true identification. As proof of this, we conclude our discussion with two sets of comparative photographs of details of two "Philadelphia Chippendale-style" chairs, one of which has only recently been deemed quite modern despite excellent craftsmanship, good faking and a genuine Randolph label glued to the inside rear rail. The details reproduced here represent areas where the deception is *not* convincing. As one focuses on these details, however, the skills and abilities represented in the falsely-old chair must be admired.

CHAPTER

15

CONCLUSIONS

WHILE ALL OF THESE thoughts may be useful, of course no proven single detail or proven single test for age is adequate for proper definition of the piece. Even a collection of "check points" will not necessarily provide the whole story; it simply helps. Sometimes evidence may be distorted, accidentally, deliberately, or simply by such events as stripping, regilding, repolishing or repairing. There are also exceptions to all rules—the sides of a chest may not be planed smooth, for example, drawer pulls may never have been put on a chest, and no two chairs will ever be exactly alike. Thus the study of antique furniture is never-ending. With constant observation and study, increasing familiarity leads to a developed instinct for what is and what is not old. This instinct is a composite of formal lessons, observation, experience, good eyes, and common sense.

Collecting old furniture is the source of much pleasure, interest and challenge to the collector. There is the pleasure of living with one's collection, a constant source of satisfaction and education. There is the pleasure of realizing that a truly fine piece of furniture will retain its aesthetic appeal as long as civilization as we know it continues. There is pleasure in the recognition that fine rare pieces will become increasingly scarce over the years, thereby rising in monetary value.

Successful collecting requires the application of all previous study, experience and training to the object under review. Perhaps the best way to approach a piece of furniture

is to develop a simple set of priorities. Probably anyone's first reaction when confronted with an unknown piece will be to try to identify its style, a subject that is beyond the scope of this text. With a tentative style dating, using criteria of size (scale and silhouette), material, decorative details and color, one then moves in closer to consider whether the piece is of the period when that style was prevalent, or whether it is a later piece in that style. Certain age characteristics will be particularly evident, and these will be the concentration, always recognizing that no detail can be relied upon in isolation. In fact, as one examines various parts of a piece, one should be on the alert for details consistent to age, or contrary-to-age. If one finds many consistent details as evidence of age (or not) one can advance a step closer to drawing a conclusion. Understanding the visible repairs and damages and their causes will help here. At this point intuition, that indefinable quality, hopefully will also reinforce one's findings. If all is still right, information about the history of the piece (its provenance) will help to confirm conclusions, and the established market price for the piece will provoke the final respect.

Careful study of dates on which new designs, decorative motifs and material were introduced is most important. Anachronisms can often be discovered when examining a suspect piece, thereby building support for its spurious status. (The basic guide for establishing the date of a piece of furniture with

169

208. *18th century American chest of drawers which has never had door pulls attached.*

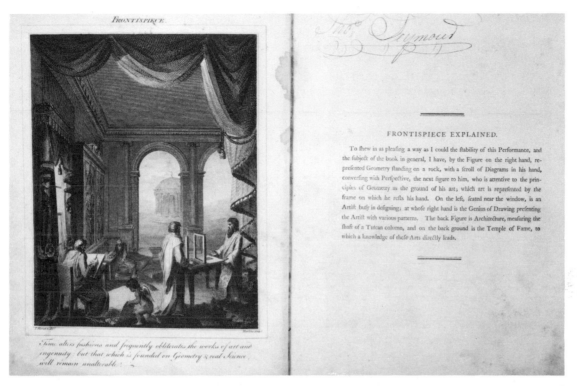

209. *Frontispiece from* The Cabinetmaker and Upholsterer's Drawing Book *in 3 parts, 1793, by Thomas Sheraton, London (1791–1793). This pattern book with the signature of Thomas Seymour on the Explanatory Leaf of the Frontispiece is the only known example of a pattern book bearing the signature of an American cabinetmaker. Seymour presumably acquired the book after 1793 while working in Boston; in 1800, Thomas became associated with his father, John Seymour, who was an outstanding cabinetmaker in Boston after the Revolution. Photograph courtesy the Museum of Fine Arts, Boston.*

characteristic features of more than one style is to use the date of the latest style detail—a cabinetmaker could work with earlier details but not those yet to be created.) It is also important to establish whether a type of furniture was popular at a particular time or even made then at all. For example, sideboards simply were not made much before 1780 in America or in England. Cabinets for the display of china were rarely made before 1715. The forger is tempted to compensate for such deficiencies.

There are several important sources of information for dating the details of an old piece of furniture. In England, records of style motifs in the 18th century are read-

ily available due to the publication of several cabinetmakers' illustrated and dated books of furniture designs—catalogs, advertisements and directories. Many large English houses are also known to have been furnished at certain dates and in some cases this documented original furniture remains in place today serving as an excellent reference source. Dyrham Park in Gloucestershire, England, is an example of this. For the most part, America was a few years behind England in style changes.

Another excellent source is in probate court inventories of the property of deceased persons. These inventories are always dated and often describe the kinds and quantities of furniture and their location in the house. Certainly royal and family coats of arms found on furniture establish provenance and sometimes actual date.

Advertisements and trade cards of cabinetmakers and shopkeepers, travel diaries, and family letters and memoirs are useful sources for documentation. Early paintings and engravings in which furniture appears are another excellent source as the piece is visible and often shown in color. John Singleton Copley's portraits (see illustration 95,

210. *The mid-18th century decorative London trade card of case and reduce cabinetmaker, John Folgham, 8⅝" by 6¼". Such a label establishes the furniture maker's address and occupation, and when the card includes engravings of furniture, the style and quality of his work can be determined. From* Sir Ambrose Heal: The London Furniture Makers, 1660–1940, *New York: Dover Publications, Inc., 1972*

211. *English dressing case circa 1800 with label of* Dobson, Hardwareman *behind inner lid (see illustration 212).*

212. *English dressing case showing label. Information about "Hardwareman Dobson" and this example of his work could likely be discovered with research into the historic records of London cabinetmaking.*

page 75) are well endowed with 18th century furniture including good detail of the materials and techniques used to cover chairs, sofas and other pieces of the time.

Evidence of date is sometimes found in printed matter glued to the piece, such as an original label of a cabinetmaker. If any record of that cabinetmaker can be found from early newspaper advertisements, directories, court entries, etc., it may be possible to establish the date of his working career. Such research may ascertain a label to be that of a later repairer whose dates may be established in a similar way or it may lead to the realization that a father and son, both cabinetmakers, had the same name and used the same label, thereby spreading the likely date range of the piece under consideration.

Rare but exciting documentary evidence for dating a piece of furniture is found in a dated bill rendered by a cabinetmaker. The furniture must be sufficiently described to connect the bill and extant place. Such bills

and documented furniture exist from the workshop of Duncan Phyfe in New York City. Harewood House in Yorkshire, England, has many bills concerning purchases of furniture for the House from the shop of Thomas Chippendale.

Dates of American furniture are sometimes suggested by the number of stars inlaid or painted on a piece. The implication here is that the number of stars indicates the number of states in the Union at the time it was made and decorated. Sometimes this correlation holds true.

Dating furniture is also done by attribution; i.e., if several pieces are found to have exactly the same characteristics, cabinet-making details and ornamental designs, and if the maker of one of them is known, all of the pieces may be attributed to that maker, thereby approximating the date of them all. The carved details of Samuel McIntire of Salem, Massachusetts—his cornucopia, basket of fruit and flowers, sheaf of wheat, and alternating flutes and rosette borders—are so well known and copied (both now and in the past) that it is uncertain and speculative to justify attribution on the basis of those details alone. In cases of attribution, caution must always be exercised.

Fashion also plays a role in collecting old furniture and, indeed, what is most fashionable dictates and realizes the highest prices. Thus the wise collector should recognize that provided a piece is appealing and a good example of its period style, truly old in itself, and in good condition, the absence of current popularity (which inflates its price) can be an advantage. Furthermore, an unfashionable piece at a low price is not likely to be faked.

Study of the marketplace for antique furniture should clarify for the collector and student alike the fact that a particularly high

213. Panel of characteristic Samuel McIntire rich carving as found on his wonderful mahogany double chest of drawers, likely made for Elizabeth Derby of Salem, Massachusetts, in 1796. Photograph courtesy the Museum of Fine Arts, Boston.

214. Backside of a looking glass frame providing information on construction, on replacement details or missing parts, and on where and how repairs have been made.

price for an object is no guarantee of its authenticity. At the same time only a dealer in stolen goods can afford to sell below market value. Forgeries are usually offered at a price sufficiently below market value to tempt the thoughtless buyer, but not so low as to be immediately suspect.

With so many details to examine and consider, perhaps it should go without saying that it is paramount to take one's time before reaching conclusions. Sit down and spend twenty minutes simply looking at the piece— how much you will glean in minute details and clues to its age. Explore the backside and underside with even greater fastidiousness. Examination of the piece in daylight out-of-doors will also reveal small details which are not easily discerned in lesser light. Physically lift the piece of furniture; an 18th century American Chippendale-style chair, for example, should be extremely heavy, since it is likely to be made of thick, heavy San Domingan mahogany. In any important decision, it is wise to confirm your conclusions with a qualified and recognized antique furniture authority.

A most valuable and wonderful way for learning about, understanding and appreciating the skills of the furniture cabinetmaker and craftsman is time actually spent in his workshop. Knowledge of methods, tools and materials used by furniture craftsmen, old and contemporary, aid the collector in protecting himself against forgeries. More important, however, is the experience of watching an expert restorer of old furniture and discussing his work with him. Respect and fascination for his capabilities, skills, and pride evolve, never to be forgotten.

GLOSSARY

A

Acanthus
A form of ornament, based on the leaves of the acanthus plant, used for the enrichment of moldings and surfaces, the knees of chairs and tables, and the arms and cresting of chairs.

Adze
A type of axe with the cutting edge at right angles to the handle. Horizontal rather than vertical strokes are used to work the adze.

Annual Rings
Concentric alternating light and dark areas, when a tree is viewed in cross section, are called annual or growth rings. A new ring appears each year representing a year's growth. The older annual rings, in the center (so-called heartwood), are usually darker and no longer function as channels of growth. The younger rings, closest to the edge (sapwood), are lighter and transport the nutrients upwards.

Apron
A shaped horizontal piece of wood below the seat rail of a chair or the frame of a case piece or table, extending between the legs, which is usually ornamented with shaping, carving, or piercing.

Astragal
A small half-round or convex bead molding.

B

Bail
A curving pull handle, often of brass, hanging from metal bolts and backed by a metal plate. As of about 1700, it was used on drawer fronts.

Banding
A narrow edging or border of veneer around the fronts of drawers, etc.; a contrasting band of inlay.

Banisters (also Balusters)
The upright turned members in a chair back or a staircase balustrade.

Bellflower
A classical style motif; flower bud of three to five narrow pointed petals, usually inlaid into veneered wood.

Bevel
A sloping edge of various angles applied to wood or glass or metal. (See Chamfer.)

Birdcage
A construction device which allows the top of a tripod table to revolve when horizontal and to be tipped up when not in use. It consists of two squares of wood connected by small turned pillars, thus resembling a birdcage. The lower square is pierced by a hole through which the pedestal is fixed by means of a wedge. The upper part is hinged to the table top by two long bearers, screwed to the underside.

Blind Tracery
Tracery carved upon a solid wooden surface, characteristic of Gothic tracery.

Block front
The front of a chest of drawers, secretary, or desk having different planes on its surface—the center section or side sections project or are recessed to achieve a contrast or blocked front. This form seems to be peculiarly American, a Baroque expression dating from the period of 1760–1780, and is associated with the work of the Goddard-Townsend School in Newport.

Bombé
The outward swelling or convex surface found on cabinets and commodes; a fashion originating in Italy and Holland which was reflected in the mid-18th century Boston-area chests of drawers and secretary-bookcases made by cabinetmakers like John Cogswell.

Bonnet Top
The curved or hooded broken Roman (arched) pediment topping tall case furniture.

Boss
A round or oval shaped wooden applied ornament, often used with applied split spindles and drops on 17th-century American case pieces and frequently painted black to suggest ebony wood.

Boulle work (or Buhl work)
The practice of inlaying brass into wood or tortoiseshell; this form of marquetry was introduced by André-Charles Boulle (1642–1732), a French cabinetmaker under the patronage of Louis XIV.

Bracket Foot
A foot shaped like a bracket, supporting chests of drawers and other case pieces, and extending a short way in both directions from the corner of the base.

Bun Foot
A foot in the form of a bun-like flattened sphere, used on chairs, tables, stands, and chests, which came into general use during the latter part of the 17th century.

Burl
An abnormal wartlike protruding growth on the trunk or branches of a tree. Examined closely, it may consist of a great mass of "eyes" or dormant buds. When sliced as a veneer it reveals beautiful figure, which was used frequently by late 17th century cabinetmakers working in the William and Mary style.

C

C-Scroll
An ornamental scroll, in the form of the letter C, often used in carved enrichment; its name derives from the Greek word cyma.

Cabinetmaker
The highly skilled and specialized maker of furniture, whose craft was created and developed by the technique of veneering, introduced into England during the second half of the 17th century. (Compare with the craft of the joiner.) The cabinetmaker became identified with fine furniture during the 18th century, and cabinetmaking has

since become a generic term for the making of furniture.

Cabochon
Carved decorative detail, resembling a cartouche, often carved on the knees of cabriole legs during the mid-18th century. Its smooth raised round or elliptical center was often surrounded by acanthus leafage.

Cabriole leg
A leg consisting of two curves, the upper part (the shoulder or knee) convex, and the lower part, above the shaped foot, concave.

Caddy (Tea Caddy)
A small box or chest often decorated with wood veneers and inlay etc. used for keeping tea, an expensive commodity in the 17th and 18th centuries. The word caddy is a corruption of catti (kāti), a weight used in the East, equal to just over a pound.

Cant
A form of chamfer or bevel, frequently used in reference to the corners of case pieces of furniture.

Carpenter
The carpenter has been concerned with structural woodwork in building, such as timber-framed roofs, since medieval times. From his craft the joiner's craft evolved.

Cartouche
A rococo decoration based on the scroll with an oval shape and curled and rolled-over edges, used frequently on mid-18th century mahogany furniture. In Philadelphia, free-standing carved cartouches were used as the center finials for tall case pieces.

Carver
Throughout furniture history the wood carver has generally worked in partnership with furniture makers, joiners or others who were responsible for making a complete object. The

carver's job was to embellish the piece in question. During the late 17th century and throughout the 18th century the carver and gilder had great independence, becoming responsible for the carving and gilding of such ornate articles as looking glass frames, console tables, candelabra and girandoles.

Caul
A stout piece of wood, slightly convex on the underside and a little larger than the panel of veneer being glued. The caul was heated and then clamped to the newly glued veneer surface for support, the heat passing through the veneers and liquefying the glue previously applied. The convex surface ensured that pressure began at the center and continued to the edges. The caul would be kept tightly in place until the glue was dry.

Chamfer
A flat surface formed by planing or flattening the angle made where two surfaces meet. (See Bevel.)

Chip carving
Simple and shallow form of carving used to decorate wooden surfaces in the 13th, 14th, and 15th centuries. The patterns, which were usually geometrical, were first set out with compasses and then chipped out with chisels and gouges, probably by the joiner who made the chest. Chip carving continued through the 16th and early 17th centuries.

Cocked Bead
A bead molding based on a semi-circular section, which projected beyond an edge or surface. It was often used in the mid-18th century around drawer fronts.

Concertina Action
A construction device often used for mid-18th century card tables with folding tops. When the moveable legs of such tables

were pulled out, the horizontal hinged frame to which they were attached straightened out and served as a support for the opened top. When the table was closed, this framing folded back like a concertina.

Counter-Boulle
Brass groundwork with tortoise-shell inlay.

Cresting
The carved decoration on the rail of a chair or settee or the back of a day bed.

Cross-banding
Border bands of veneer in which the grain runs across the band. This decorative banding was characteristic of late 17th and early 18th century veneered furniture.

Cross-grain molding
A molding with the grain of the wood running across its width and not along its length. Cross-grained moldings were a characteristic feature of walnut furniture in the late 17th century and early part of the 18th century.

Crotch
The place in a tree where the main stem (or large branch) forks to produce two smaller stems. Crotch figure wood is obtained from wood directly below the bifurcation and is the result of the division of the stem.

D

Diaper
Decoration consisting of repetitions of small squares or lozenges, etc., forming an all-over pattern on a surface. This form of repeating pattern is used in marquetry, and for low relief carving in wood and gesso.

Drop-leaf
A table with hinged leaves that can be raised to enlarge it. Supports for the leaves are either legs or other supports swung into position. Such tables include butterfly tables, corner tables, gateleg tables, and so-called Pembroke tables.

E

Ébénistes
Members of French guilds who faced the surfaces of their furniture with veneers of precious wood (no longer necessarily ebony, origin of the word in 17th century). Furniture treated in this way was confined to chests of drawers, desks and tables. The term ébéniste goes back no farther than the second half of the 17th century when furniture veneered with ebony became popular with well-to-do people. Later on, in the 18th century when more colorful woods were largely substituted for ebony, men so engaged still called themselves ébénistes. Thus, furniture by the master ébéniste means furniture dating from the latter part of the 17th century to the close of the 18th century when the cabinet-makers' guilds were abolished by law.

Escutcheon
Ornamental key plate, usually brass, placed over and surrounding the keyhole.

F

Facing
A term in furniture construction meaning a thin covering of wood, such as mahogany, not necessarily a veneer, upon a ground of secondary wood. The expression faced-up is a reference to this.

Figure
The natural decorative marking or pattern seen on the surface of cut wood. This pattern is not the grain of the wood but rather its figure. Figure results from the interaction of several features present in the wood—for example, the presence or absence of growth rings, the prominence of and abundance of vascular rays, and local variations in color due to uneven deposition of coloring substances in wood. Strikingly beautiful patterns are exhibited in the wood from the vicinity of crotches, and burls form interesting natural designs or figures.

Finial
Carved or brass terminal ornament projecting upward from the cornice or pediment of a case piece (such as a high chest of drawers or a clock case). Finials also terminate the tops of chair uprights.

Flitch
A section of log which has been sawn into a bundle of consecutive sheets of veneer.

Fluting
Shallow concave grooves on a surface are called flutes, and flutes used in vertical parallel series are known as fluting—such as the fluting on a column or a chair leg. Fluting was an important detail used in ancient classical architecture on columns and pilasters and was used for furniture parts during the late 18th century classical revival style. Good flutes are close together and deep with a sharply scooped curve for the ending; the ridge between the flutes is called a fillet.

French Foot
A bracket foot which curves outward as it nears the floor.

French Polish
A finish introduced and used extensively in the 19th century in which a polish was produced by treating the surface of the wood with shellac in spirit, the process being to build up layer upon layer of the shellac until the desired depth and quality

of gloss was achieved. A perfect mirror finish was the goal.

G

Gadrooning
A carved ornamental edging of a repeating pattern—curving alternating convex and concave sections. This detail was particularly popular on furniture in New York during the mid-18th century.

Gateleg
A form of drop-leaf table with swinging supports that are legs joined to the main frame of the table by upper and lower stretchers which make a gate. These swinging supports were used for gateleg tables in the late 17th century and early 18th century.

Gesso
A composition of a white material (usually gypsum or whiting), linseed oil and glue. It was used either as a ground for paintings or as a surface treatment for plain or carved wood upon which was laid a metallic leaf such as gold or paint.

Gilding
The decoration of surfaces with applied gold leaf or gold dust is known as gilding. The practice of gilding furniture, particularly the stands of cabinets, became popular in the time of Charles II in England, and there was a revival of the use of this form of decoration in the early Georgian Period. Thomas Sheraton in *The Cabinet Dictionary* (1803), defines gilding as "the art of spreading or covering thin gold over any substance."

Girandole
A circular convex looking-glass with candle brackets as part of the decorative frame.

Gouge
A hollow chisel used by cabinet-makers and carvers.

Gouge Work
The name given to gouge carving, a rudimentary form of surface decoration achieved by scooping out regularly spaced shallow depressions with a gouge. The resulting pattern was a kind of fluting, used during the late 16th and 17th centuries.

Grain
Wood grain refers to the direction or orientation of wood cells, particularly the fibrous elements. Thus straight grain occurs when the fibers and other longitudinally oriented elements are more or less parallel to the vertical axis of the trunk, and irregular grain is produced in timber where the fibers are at varying and irregular inclinations to the vertical axis of a log (often in the region of knots or swollen butts).

Graining
The highly skilled imitation of the color and wood grain (thus figure) of a costly wood, achieved with paint on the surface of a less interesting and expensive wood. This was first done in England at the end of the 16th century for the imitation of oak and walnut.

H

Hardwoods
Woods supplied from broad-leaved trees, belonging to the botanical group Angiosperms.

Hasp
Hinged part of a hinge lock such as the elaborate iron locks found on 15th century European chests.

Herringbone
Patterns in the form of herringbone (alternately slanting grain) were used as banding on early 18th century walnut veneered furniture.

Hinge
A folding metal joint by which doors, lids etc. swing on a pivot center.

I

Inlay
A method of decorating a solid wood surface, by which decorative cuts are made into the wooden ground and these cuts or grooves are filled with other materials, either woods of different colors or metal, ivory, or mother-of-pearl.

Intarsia (*or Tarsia*)
A term of Renaissance Italy origin to describe inlay patterns especially of wood. This work, often of a geometric or pictorial nature, was in the form of panels for walls or incorporated into furniture.

J

Japanning
European and American imitation of Oriental lacquer work, using layers of paint and varnish with raised plaster Chinoiserie designs. This technique was popular in late 17th century England and America. A book of instructions, *Treatise of Japanning and Varnishing* by Stalker and Parker, was published in 1688 in London.

Joiner
The craft of the joiner, or "joyner," evolved from carpentry. The joiner handled woodwork that was smaller in scale than structural woodwork, which was the carpenter's province, and he developed a careful and exacting technique, based upon firmness and accuracy, in the making of mortise and tenon joints plus skill in smoothing solid wood surfaces.

Joinery
The technique of joining together pieces of solid wood.

K

Knee
The upper convex curve or bulge of a cabriole leg.

Kneehole
The opening between the two banks of drawers constructed for certain desks, allowing room for the sitter's knees.

Knot
Cross section of a branch or limb at the point where a limb emerges from a tree trunk.

L

Lathe
A machine for shaping turned parts which holds the revolving wood during applications of the chisel cutting edge.

Linenfold Panel
(or Parchment Panel)
A form of ornament used on wall panelling and the panels of chests and on chair backs during the early 16th century, consisting of vertical mouldings terminating in folds. The design may have originally been suggested by folded linen or by scrolls of parchment. It was of Continental origin, probably from Flanders, and came to England at the end of the 15th century.

Lopers
An English term for the sliding rails or arms which pull out from the frame of a slant-top desk or secretary to support the fall or drop-front.

M

Masterpiece
Piece of work by which a craftsman apprentice gained from his guild the recognized rank of "master" craftsman.

Menuisier
Woodworker in solid wood ornamented with carving. Pieces of furniture thus produced were cupboards, side tables (consoles), chairs and beds.

Mirror
The word mirror first meant a hand mirror or any reflecting surface, and early mirrors, dating back to ancient history in China and Egypt, were of polished metal. When glass was coated with amalgam of mercury, the term looking glass, or glass, replaced mirror. It was not until the late 19th century that the word mirror came back into general use, and was applied to all forms of looking glasses.

Molding
A continuous band projection or incision, curved or faceted in section, or with combined curves and facets, used as a decorative band.

Mortise
Oblong square hole or slot cut by a chisel made for that purpose, which is designed to receive a projecting piece of wood called a tenon to form a joint, the so-called mortise and tenon joint.

N

Nulling
A form of carved decoration of alternating concave and convex flutes, sometimes described as gadrooning, used on the flat or molded edges of tables and cabinet stands etc. in the 17th and 18th centuries.

O

Ogee
The common name for the molding known in classical architecture as cyma recta. In section it has a double curve, concave above and convex below.

Ogee Reversed
The common name for the molding in classical architecture known as cyma reversa. In section it has a double curve, convex above, concave below. The 18th century ogee bracket foot is in fact a reverse ogee curve.

Ormolu
An alloy of copper, zinc, and tin (bronze) which is gilded and used for decorative mounts on furniture. Its use is associated chiefly with the ornate furniture made in France during the 18th century, and in France these mounts are described as bronze doré (gilded bronze).

Ovolo
A wide convex molding, used both for architecture and cabinet making, which is quarter round in section being a quadrant of a circle.

P

Panel
A sunken or raised surface, framed by the grooved stiles and rails of a door, or the front or lid of a chest.

Parcel Gilt
Partly gilded. Carved mahogany mid-18th century looking glass frames, for example, often have parts picked out (high-lighted) with gilding, hence the frame is parcel gilt.

Pediment
An architectural term for a triangular or curved form above the upper member of a classical cornice. The pediment was sometimes used on late 17th century bookcases and frequently in many forms (Greek and Roman broken pediments and pierced pediments) on 18th century large architectural pieces such as library bookcases, cabinets and high chests of drawers. (When "broken," the lines of the pediment are stopped short before reaching the apex.)

Pendant
A term that applies to a variety of furniture ornaments all of which hang down or drop.

Pietra-Dura
A form of ornamental mosaic work introduced in 16th Century Renaissance Italy which consisted of hard stones, such as agate, lapis lazuli, jasper, and fragments of precious marbles, inlaid into a surface and highly polished. Table tops and decorative cabinets of that period were often so ornamented.

Pilaster
An architectural vertical detail, rectangular in section, projecting slightly from the surface, though attached, and reproducing the characteristic proportions of a base column and capital in one of the orders of architecture. Pilasters were an important feature of 18th century cabinetwork.

Pollard oak (also walnut, poplar, willow and elm)
A dark brown wood with a wavy grain, which is supplied from oak trees that have been "polled" and their growth arrested. Pollarding involves the removal of the crown or top branches of a tree, leaving the main stem intact.

Q

Quadrant
Metal device, usually brass, of quarter-circle shape used to support some fall-front desks of late 18th and 19th century construction.

R

Rail
The horizontal members in the frame of a case piece or panelling. The horizontal members of a table or chair frame are also known as rails.

Rebate (or Rabbet)
A continuous rectangular channel or sinking, cut along the edge of a piece of wood or framework.

Reeding
The decoration of a surface by a series of parallel convex half-round moldings of equal width. Sheraton in his 1803 *Cabinet Dictionary* speaks of reeding as a mode by which table legs, bed pillars, etc., are ornamented, and as one of the most substantial kinds of ornament yet adopted. "It is much preferable to fluting or cabling in point of strength; and in look, much superior to the latter; and almost the only ornament that has escaped the notice of the ancients, as I do not recollect any instance of reeding in any part of ancient architecture. When reeding is introduced on flat surfaces, there ought always to be 3, 5, 7, and so on, and the odd one should be in the center."

Rococo
The word rococo derives from the French word *rocaille* which means "rock-work," a term used originally to describe the artificial grottos and fountains in the gardens of Versailles. The rococo style developed in France during the early part of the Louis XV Period and it reached England in the mid-18th century, influencing Thomas Chippendale and his contemporaries. The style was exuberant, light, graceful, and asymmetrical, intermingling ornamental forms of foliage, shells, scrolls, and acanthus leaves.

Rottenstone
Soft, finely powdered stone used with oil to polish wood furniture surfaces.

S

S-Scroll
Ornamental detail, often carved, in an S-shape, based on the cyma recta and cyma reversa curves of ancient classical architecture.

Saddle seat
Chair seat scooped away to the sides and back from a central ridge, resembling the pommel of a saddle. Windsor chair seats frequently have saddle seats for more comfortable sitting.

Scratch carving
The simplest form of incised carving, consisting of single lines scratched in the surface of woodwork with a V-chisel. Such carving is found on early 17th century pieces.

Scratch stock
A simple tool for working moldings, inlays, etc. in which an adjustable cutter of thin steel is held between two pieces of wood screwed together and notched at one end. Scraping or scratching action across the wood cuts the molding, and depth is controlled by the top of the notch bearing down on the surface of the wood.

Serpentine Front
A convex curve flanked by two concave curves, used on the fronts of chests of drawers, commodes and sideboards, which first appeared in the mid-18th century.

Slip-seat
A separate upholstered wood frame seat which lets into the primary wood framing of the chair seat.

Splat
The central vertical member between the uprights of a chair back, often pierced and/or shaped.

Splay
The outward spread or slope of a surface or a leg. A French foot is a form of splayed foot.

Split spindles
Vertically halved spindles (or balusters) turned and then separated and applied as decoration to 17th century oak furniture. Split spindles are also used

for chair backs with the smooth side to the sitter's back.

Stiles
The vertical or upright members in the panel frame of a door or case piece into which the horizontal members (rails) are fitted. The vertical members of a chairback are also stiles.

Strapwork
A form of decoration used on late 16th and 17th century furniture consisting of flat interlacing carved bands (or straps) and turned balusters and bosses, split and applied to the stiles and rails of chests and cupboards.

Stretcher
Horizontal rails or bars which connect the legs of stools, chairs, tables, and stands for chests, providing a strengthening function. In the late 17th century the stretcher also became a decorative feature for chairs and tables. Although it survived during the 18th century, its use was discontinued by fashionable cabinetmakers towards the end of that century.

Stringing
The inlaying of narrow strips of contrasting colored wood. Woods frequently used for stringing were holly, satinwood, boxwood and ebony.

Style
Description of the design and ornamental details characteristic of the furniture of any given time, place, person or group. A style may be interpreted in varied ways in other countries or times.

Swage block
An iron block containing holes and grooves of various sizes used for heading bolts and shaping objects not easily worked on an anvil.

T

Tambour
Doors made of flexible sliding panels operating horizontally or vertically made by gluing thin strips of wood to a linen background. (These run in a groove and may follow any shape.) This detail was favored in Louis XVI work and exploited by the Seymour cabinetmakers of Boston.

Tang
A projecting metal shank or tongue which serves as a connector. Used most often in the furniture context in reference to case piece brass mounts—a tang running from the front to the inside through the mount holds the mount in place.

Templet
A flat pattern or outline cut out of thin wood or card for each part to be joined into a piece of furniture. For a Queen Anne chair, there would be templets for front and back legs, the arms and their supports, a splat, top rail and seat rails. The templetes for that chair would be tied together in a bundle and these bundles usually were stored by being hung high on the walls of cabinetmaking shops.

Tenon
A rectangular projection carved at the end of a chair rail, for example, which conforms in size and shape to fit into a carved recess (the mortise), thereby forming the strong mortise and tenon joint.

Tracheid Vessels
Vessels in a tree which carry the sap from the roots to the leaves and constitute the "grain" of a cut board.

Turnery
The craft of shaping wood by using cutting chisels upon a rotating surface. The device for rotating, or turning, the wood is called a lathe. Baluster turning resulted in turned members of various columnar shapes; ball and spool turning and bobbin turning imitated the shapes of spools or bobbins; twist and spiral turning were other popular 17th century characteristic turnings.

U

Undercut
A term used to describe deeply carved ornamental woodwork where parts of the carved ornament are separated from the ground or the molded surface.

V

Veneer
Wood cut into extremely thin sheets, or any thin sheet(s) of material, such as ivory or tortoiseshell, glued to the furniture core for decorative effect.

Veneering
The highly skilled craft of applying thin sheets of wood or other decorative materials to a surface. The object of veneering was sometimes economy and sometimes appearance. The cost of the core wood plus the glue and the extra time involved, however, often made this process as expensive as the use of solid woods.

Vernis Martin
A generic name for a particularly brilliant translucent lacquer used for the decoration of furniture and interiors in 18th Century France. The four Martin brothers, beginning as coach painters, developed a method of lacquering (patent 1730, renewed 1744) which brought them Court patronage and widespread fame. They used many

colors but their green lacquer was the most famous.

W

Wainscot
Name originally used in medi-aeval England for imported wood suitable for wagon (wain) construction, and thus for furniture and panelling.

Water leaf
A carved ornamental motif of a narrow leaf with regular horizontal undulations divided by the stem going down the center. It was used in the early 19th century classical style and favored by Duncan Phyfe as a leg decoration.

SELECTED BIBLIOGRAPHY

Bjerkoe, Ethel Hall. *The Cabinetmakers of America.* Garden City: Doubleday & Co., 1957.

Bridenbaugh, Carl. *The Colonial Craftsman.* New York: New York University Press, 1950.

Cescinsky, Herbert. *The Gentle Art of Faking Furniture.* New York: Dover Publications, 1968.

Constantine, Jr., Albert. *Know Your Woods.* 4th ed. New York: Albert Constantine & Son, Inc., 1969.

Crawley, W., *Is It Genuine?* London: Eyre & Spottiswoode, 1971.

DeBles, Arthur. *Genuine Antique Furniture.* New York: Thomas Y. Crowell Co., 1929.

Fales, Dean A. Jr. *American Painted Furniture 1660–1880.* New York: Dutton, 1972.

Hayward, Charles H. *Antique or Fake? The Making of Old Furniture.* London: Evans Brothers Ltd., 1970.

————. *Furniture Repairs.* London: Evans Brothers Ltd., 1967.

Hinckley, F. Lewis. *Directory of the Historic Cabinet Woods.* New York: Crown Publishers, Inc., 1960.

Hornor, William MacPherson, Jr. *Blue Book, Philadelphia Furniture.* Bryn Mawr: The Author, 1935.

Hummel, Charles F. *With Hammer in Hand. The Dominy Craftsmen of East Hampton, New York.* Charlottesville: University Press of Virginia, 1968.

Joyce, Ernest. *The Technique of Furniture Making.* London: B. T. Batford Ltd., 1970.

Kirk, John T. *American Chairs.* New York: Alfred A. Knopf, 1972.

————. *Early American Furniture. How to Recognize, Evaluate, Buy and Care for the Most Beautiful Pieces—High-Style, Country, Primitive and Rustic.* New York: Alfred A. Knopf, 1970.

Kurz, Otto. *Fakes, A Handbook for Collectors and Students.* 2nd ed. revised and enlarged. New York: Dover Publications, 1967.

Marsh, Moreton. *The Easy Expert in Collecting and Restoring American Antiques.* Philadelphia and New York: J. B. Lippincott Co., 1959.

Macquoid, Percy, and Edwards, Ralph. *Dictionary of English Furniture.* 3 vols. New York: Scribner, 1924.

Mercer, Henry C. *Ancient Carpenters' Tools.* Doylestown, Penn.: The Bucks County Historical Society, 1951.

Mills, John Fitzmaurice. *The Care of Antiques.* New York: Hastings House, 1964.

Ormsbee, Thomas H. *Care and Repair of Antiques.* New York: Medill McBride Co., 1949.

Pinto, Edward H. *The Craftsman in Wood.* London: G. Bell and Sons, Ltd., 1962.

Rodd, John. *The Repair and Restoration of Furniture.* New York: Charles Scribner's Sons, 1955.

Sack, Albert. *Fine Points of Furniture: Early American.* New York: Crown Publishers, 1950.

Savage, George. *Forgeries, Fakes, and Reproductions: A Handbook for the Art Dealer and Collector.* New York: Praeger, 1963.

Symonds, R. W. *Old English Walnut and Lacquer Furniture: The Present-Day Condition and Value and the Methods of the Furniture-Faker in Producing Spurious Pieces.* New York: Robert M. McBride & Co., 1923.

Wildung, Frank H. *Woodworking Tools at the Shelburne Museum.* Museum Pamphlet Series No. 3. Shelburne, Va.: The Shelburne Museum, 1957.

Yates, Raymond F. *Antique Fakes And Their Detection.* New York: Harper & Bros. Publishers, 1950.

185

INDEX